Voices for the Culture of Peace

Voices *for* the Culture *of* Peace

Compendium of the
SGI-USA Culture of Peace
Distinguished Speaker Series

VOLUME 3

Culture of Peace Press

Published by Culture of Peace Press
An imprint of the SGI-USA
606 Wilshire Blvd., Santa Monica, CA 90401

© 2016 SGI-USA

Printed in the United States of America.

Cover and interior design by VJB/Scribe.

Volume 1 ISBN: 978-0-9844050-0-8
Volume 2 ISBN: 978-0-9844050-4-6
Volume 3 ISBN: 978-0-9844050-8-4

LIBRARY OF CONGRESS CATALOGING-IN-PUBLICATION DATA

Voices for a culture of peace: compendium of the SGI-USA Culture of Peace
distinguished speakers series.
v. <1-> ; cm.
Includes bibliographical references and index.
ISBN 978-0-9844050-0-8 (alk. paper)
1. Peace. 2. Peace-building. 3. Peace — Religious aspects — Buddhism. I. Soka Gakkai
International-USA. II. Title.
JZ5538.V65 2010
303.6'6 — dc22

2009054135

10 9 8 7 6 5 4 3 2 1

CONTENTS

Disarmament, Moral Leadership, and the Culture of Peace

Sergio de Queiroz Duarte

Former United Nations High Representative for
Disarmament Affairs

Those who take the time to walk around the grounds of the United Nations Headquarters in New York will have the opportunity to see many visual images that relate to the lofty ideals that presided over the founding of this great institution, as recorded in its charter. Let me recall just one of those ideals, namely the determination of "the peoples of the United Nations" to "unite our strength to maintain international peace and security."

Among the visual reminders of this pledge that a visitor will see is a large pistol with its barrel tied into a knot. One will see Saint George slaying a dragon whose body is made out of parts of dismantled missiles. One will see a giant hammering a huge sword into a plowshare and upon crossing First Avenue he may read the words "nation shall not lift up sword against nation, neither shall they learn war any more" inscribed on a wall. Other works of art displayed throughout the building also may inspire the visitor to reflect on the theme of peace: a giant cube made of seven thousand small arms welded together, an electric guitar made from an AK-47 rifle, and an ingenious exhibit from Mozambique titled Arms for Art, with statues and even furniture made of weapons parts. On the occasion of the environmental gathering of Rio + 20, in my native city of Rio de Janeiro, the public was able to gaze at a battle tank covered with bread, underscoring the ever recurrent theme of the need to channel resources used for destruction into projects designed to alleviate the basic needs of men, women, and children in the most underdeveloped parts of the world.

Dag Hammarskjold, one of the greatest Secretaries-General who served the United Nations, once said: "The pursuit of peace and progress cannot end in a few years in either victory or defeat. The pursuit of peace and progress, with its trials and its errors, its successes and its setbacks, can never be relaxed and never abandoned."

These words are in line with the ideas expressed by the distinguished individuals who have addressed audiences through the SGI-USA Culture of Peace Distinguished Speaker Series. Some of their outstanding contributions to the endeavor of spreading the culture of peace are recorded in the pages of *Voices for the Culture of Peace*, vol. 3. Themes such as the role of women as peacebuilders, the pursuit of peace at the individual level, the relationship between human rights and a culture of peace, gender equality, climate change, and the sustainability of mankind, to name just a few, are among the issues highlighted in this volume. The need for a dialogue for disarmament also stands out as an essential element of the culture of peace.

A large part of my professional life as a diplomat has been devoted precisely to the task of promoting a dialogue conducive to the achievement of the goal of disarmament, particularly with regard to weapons of mass destruction. The United Nations Charter came into being before any nuclear weapon had ever been tested. The first resolution of the United Nations, adopted in January 1946, included the elimination of nuclear weapons and "all other weapons adaptable to mass destruction" as a goal to be pursued by its Member States. Over the course of several decades, mankind has banned, through a number of treaties and institutions, two categories of weapons of mass destruction: biological and chemical. Only one category of such arms remains — atomic weapons — defying the ingenuity and hard work of many dedicated men and women who have given the best of their effort to the achievement of nuclear disarmament.

What immediately stands out in this endeavor is that the goal of disarmament is truly universal in scope and emanates from recommendations and binding commitments that have been accepted by all Member States. The goal is not to outlaw certain weapons only in some countries while certifying their legitimacy elsewhere. The norms that result from this collective work seek to advance the concrete self-interest of Member

States through their very function of serving the interests of all humanity. Secretary-General Ban Ki-moon has often referred to disarmament and nonproliferation of weapons of mass destruction as "a global public good" precisely because its benefits are indivisible and enjoyed by all Member States of the United Nations — indeed by all people on our planet.

It is in the interest of the very survival of humanity that nuclear weapons are never used again, under any circumstances. No nation has the capacity to address adequately the catastrophic effects of a nuclear weapon detonation, whether by accident, miscalculation, or design. The only way to avert the dangers inherent in defense doctrines based on the possibility of the use of nuclear weapons is their complete elimination.

Disarmament represents the fusion of idealism and realism — it is the right thing to do, and it works. The objective is not a world in which fewer nuclear weapons remain in fewer hands, but a world in which such weapons do not exist. The objective is not the mere reduction of the risk that weapons of mass destruction may be used, but to eliminate both the possibility and the motivations for any such use. The objective is not to limit the damage from a future nuclear war, but to achieve a world in which such a war cannot occur. This is the true meaning of the effort to build the culture of peace.

The diversity of people who have supported these objectives and promoted these lofty goals has always impressed me in my work. Arms races and military competition may produce material benefits for certain constituencies in society, but disarmament produces benefits that cut across all sectors of human societies. All the great goals that the United Nations has been pursuing for sixty-nine years — the reduction of poverty, the protection of the environment, the promotion of justice, the defense of the dignity of the human individual — all these tacitly assume the absence of a nuclear war. In a very real sense, this involves not just humanity as a whole, but future generations as well.

The objectives encompassed in the culture of peace refer to legitimate ends — goals that are both fair and adopted through an open process of voluntary consent. This means something quite beyond simply ensuring the triumph of right over might. It involves the capability to inspire the mighty to pursue righteous ends as much as it involves efforts by the mighty to pursue such ends through collective action. It involves moral leadership that is not limited to any given level of government: it can be exercised by city mayors, legislators, civil servants, members of nongovernmental organizations — indeed, and above all, by ordinary citizens, who are the promoters and final beneficiaries of the results of the spread and practice of the culture of peace.

Moral leadership requires a troubled conscience, dissatisfaction with the status quo, and a profound sense of repugnance for all actions that rob the individual human being of his or her dignity, but also requires the hopeful vision of a better world, an awareness of the concrete and spiritual benefits of achieving a world free of all weapons of mass slaughter, and an appreciation that we will together leave for future generations a world that is safer and more peaceful than the imperfect one we share today. In short, it both requires and promotes the culture of peace.

Ian McIlraith

Director, SGI-USA Peace and Community Relations

S GI-USA is proud to publish this third volume of Voices for the Culture of Peace featuring talks delivered in our Distinguished Speaker Series. Our focus for these lectures continues to be one or more of the action areas defined in the 1999 United Nations Declaration and Programme of Action on a Culture of Peace, namely: (1) Fostering a culture of peace through education, (2) Promoting sustainable economic and social development, (3) Promoting respect for all human rights, (4) Ensuring equality between women and men, (5) Fostering democratic participation, (6) Advancing understanding, tolerance, and solidarity, (7) Supporting participatory communication and the free flow of information and knowledge, and (8) Promoting international peace and security.

We are extremely fortunate yet again to have one more preeminent champion of the culture of peace contribute the introduction to this volume, Sergio de Queiroz Duarte, former United Nations High Representative for Disarmament Affairs.

I hope the reader finds this to be another series of stimulating and thoughtful talks on this important subject. They certainly represent a variety of disciplines and perspectives that touch the Culture of Peace from different directions and hopefully epitomize the wider dialogue we intend to stimulate with this speaker series as well as these publications.

While the SGI-USA does not necessarily endorse all of the ideas or views expressed by each speaker in this series, we do hope they awaken the peacebuilder within each person who hears or reads them. Ultimately, we want increasing numbers of people to realize that the true culture of peace requires active engagement by all citizens, all organizations, and all institutions.

On behalf of the SGI-USA, I must once again express appreciation to former United Nations Under-Secretary-General Anwarul K. Chowdhury. He inaugurated this speaker series at the SGI-USA New York Culture Center in July 2007 and has consistently provided encouragement and wise guidance for these publications as well as the speaker series. Finally, we remain deeply indebted to the president of the Soka Gakkai International, Daisaku Ikeda, for his decades of leadership and example as an individual working to fulfill humankind's shared desire for the global culture of peace.

The Culture of Peace — Essence of a New Global Civilization

Ambassador Anwarul K. Chowdhury

Under-Secretary-General and High Representative of the
United Nations (2002–2007)

In July 2007, I had the pleasure and honor of launching the SGI-USA's Culture of Peace Distinguished Speaker Series in New York. Now this series is also held regularly in Los Angeles, New York, and Washington, D.C. Occasional lectures as a part of this series are also held in Honolulu and Chicago. These five SGI-USA Culture of Peace Resource Centers, as well as the sixth that opened in February 2013 in San Francisco, contribute in a significant way to spread the essential message of the culture of peace and to empower people toward self-transformation — individually and collectively — to embrace peace and nonviolence as part of their human existence.

I extend my heartfelt recognition of the tremendous success of the speaker series and its significant role in raising awareness of the multidimensional perspective of the culture of peace. The activities of each resource center also deserve our wholehearted appreciation. I believe this lecture series will become a very important landmark in the history of the SGI-USA's remarkable efforts in promoting the culture of peace, far beyond just being a number of lectures by eminent personalities.

In its essence the culture of peace transcends all boundaries and differences. It transcends differences in age and differences in culture or language or ethnicity or history. It is the most universal thing that one can internalize. My deep, sincere appreciation goes to the Soka Gakkai International in particular for giving this special profile to the global movement for the culture of peace, as called for by the United Nations General Assembly resolutions over the years. The international community as a whole owes the SGI and its president, Daisaku Ikeda, a great deal for championing this cause of global peace and human empowerment.

The publication of this third volume in the series at this time is very relevant as the drums of war are being sounded now. Peace-loving peoples of the world are holding their breath and praying intensely that another avoidable war does not break out.

It is my faith that the values of nonviolence, tolerance, and democracy which augment the flourishing of the culture of peace will generate the mindset that is a prerequisite for the transition from force to reason, from conflict and violence to dialogue and peace.

My work took me to the farthest corners of the world. From Sierra Leone to Sri Lanka, from Mongolia to Mauritius, from Paraguay to the Philippines, from Kosovo to Kazakhstan, from Bhutan to the Bahamas to Burkina Faso, I have seen time and again how people — even the humblest and the weakest — have contributed to building the culture of peace in their personal lives, in their families, in their communities, and in their countries — all these contributing to global peace one way or the other.

One lesson that I have learned from this is that we should never forget that when women — half of the world's seven plus billion people — are marginalized, there is no chance for our world to get sustainable peace in the real sense.

While women are often the first victims of armed conflict, they must also and always be recognized as key to the resolution of the conflict. It is my strong belief that unless women are engaged in advancing the culture of peace at equal levels with men, sustainable peace would continue to elude us.

As I have reiterated time and again, without peace, development is impossible and without development, peace is not achievable, but without women, neither peace nor development is possible.

In recent times, we have seen new conflicts breaking out in different parts of the world. Obviously, we have to find better ways to establish peace. We need to remember that in the hate and violence that filled the twentieth century, we have seen the power of nonviolence in the sacrifices of Mohandas Gandhi, Martin Luther King Jr., and Nelson Mandela. Forces of hatred and intolerance finally claimed their lives ... but not their souls, not their ideals.

In this context, let me also express my concern that continuing an ever-expanding militarism and militarization are impoverishing and maiming both the earth and humanity. Our planet and its people are being overwhelmed by this expansion and feeling a sense of helplessness to stall this juggernaut. Most of the problems challenging our peace, development, and human rights are caused by militarism with its blinding faith in the efficacy of force and power.

The culture of peace should be the foundation of the new global society. In today's world, more so, it should be seen as the essence of a new humanity, a new global civilization based on inner oneness and outer diversity.

We should not isolate peace as something separate or distant. We should know how to relate to one another without being aggressive, without being violent, without being disrespectful, without neglect, without prejudice. It is important to realize that the absence of peace takes away the opportunities that we need to better ourselves, to prepare ourselves, to empower ourselves to face the challenges of our lives, individually and collectively.

In this context, a critical dimension is worthy of our particular attention. Poverty and lack of opportunities deprive people of their dignity as human beings, leaving them hopeless and incapable of pursuing the kind of lives they may deserve. We must not forget that it is not only morally unsupportable but also practically unrealistic to achieve sustainable peace without addressing squarely the crushing problems of poverty and human insecurity.

It is, therefore, absolutely essential that human security in a broader sense should receive priority attention of the international community. "Peace does not mean just to stop wars, but also to stop oppression, injustice, and neglect."

How can we build the culture of peace? In 1999, the United Nations General Assembly adopted by consensus the Declaration and Programme of Action on a Culture of Peace, a monumental document aimed at guiding our people and planet to have a better future. It was an honor for me to chair the nine-month long negotiations, which led to the adoption of this historic, norm-setting, life-transforming document. Though this landmark Programme of Action is an agreement among nations, it is governments, civil society, media, individuals, and obviously, the United Nations that are all identified in this document as key actors in the accompanying declaration.

U.N. Secretary-General Ban Ki-moon asserted at the inaugural U.N. High Level Forum on the Culture of Peace in 2012 that "a key ingredient in building a culture of peace is education. We are here to talk about how to create this culture of peace. I have a simple, one-word answer: education. Through education, we teach children not to hate. Through education, we raise leaders who act with wisdom and compassion. Through education, we establish a true, lasting culture of peace."

All educational institutions need to offer opportunities that prepare the students not only to live fulfilling lives but also to be responsible and productive citizens of the world. Indeed, this should be more appropriately called "education for global citizenship." Such learning cannot be achieved without well-intentioned, sustained, and systematic peace education that leads the way to the culture of peace.

Energized by the positive outcome of the Forum in 2012, the U.N. General Assembly in its resolution on the implementation of its Programme of Action requested the president of the U.N. General Assembly to convene the High Level Forum every year on or around September 13, the date of its adoption of the Programme in 1999. As a result, the Forum was convened by the subsequent presidents in 2013 and 2014 and hopefully will continue in every coming year.

Albert Einstein once said, "The world is a dangerous place to live, not because of the people who are evil, but because of the people who don't do anything about it."

Let us not sit back any more, lulled by a sense of complacency. The time to act is NOW.

Let us send a strong, loud, and clear message to all that there is no place for war in our world.

Let us embrace the culture of peace for the good of humanity, for the sustainability of our planet, and for making our world a better place.

I am confident that as you read this third volume of the collection of lectures from the SGI-USA Culture of Peace Distinguished Speaker

Series, you will be motivated and energized to take actions and do things irrespective of your personal or professional pursuits and wherever you are to create the culture of peace in your life and those of the others.

For that, as readers of this volume, you deserve a big "thank you" from all of us!

From Former Child Soldier to Human Rights Activist

Ishmael Beah

Ishmael Beah was born in Sierra Leone on November 23, 1980. When he was eleven, his life, along with the lives of millions of other Sierra Leoneans, was derailed by the outbreak of a brutal civil war. After Ishmael's parents and two brothers were killed, he was recruited to fight as a child soldier. He was thirteen. Ishmael fought for more than two years before he was removed from the army by UNICEF and placed in a rehabilitation home in Freetown, capital of Sierra Leone. After completing rehabilitation in late 1996, Ishmael won a competition to attend a conference at the United Nations to talk about the devastating effects of war on children in his country. It was there that he met his new mother, a professional storyteller who lived in New York City. Ishmael returned to Sierra Leone and continued speaking about his experiences to help bring international attention to the issue of child soldiering and war-affected children.

In 1998, Ishmael came to live with his American family in New York City. He completed high school at the U.N. International School and went on to Oberlin College. Throughout his education, Ishmael continued his advocacy work on behalf of children affected by war, speaking at UNICEF Human Rights Watch, U.N. Secretary-General's Office for Children and Armed Conflict, U.N. General Assembly.

Ishmael Beah is a member of the Human Rights Watch Children's Rights Division Committee and the best-selling author of *A Long Way Gone: Memoirs of a Boy Soldier*.

Ishmael Beah's work addresses many of the eight action areas in the 1999 United Nations Declaration and Programme of Action on a Culture of Peace, most significantly the third: Promoting respect for all human rights. As he says: "It is essential to promote and respect human rights and respect everyone's life. We need to be able not only to see people's humanity but to learn to forgive and more important to learn to expose ourselves to the world and learn about other people's lives, other people's cultures, beyond our environment.... When we do so, I believe it will be difficult to make a case for war."

The need to promote respect for all human rights is what I'm going to focus on, interspersing my story between that.

When I was in high school, I think it was a mutual understanding between the school and my [adoptive] mother, Laura Sims, and myself that we shouldn't discuss my background with everyone; not because I was ashamed of it, but because I felt that it wasn't a story that you can tell parents or students in a very short time over lunch at a cafeteria, like, "So, you know, I used to be in this war." I think, if parents have learned just briefly about it without the entire story, they would have probably gotten very worried about my presence in the school. For everyone's sanity, we decided to leave it the way it was.

In school, I was friends with lots of people but I always tried not to say much about myself. Every question that I was asked, I gave an answer that didn't leave room for further questioning. When people met my mom, who is a white American, they said, "So, you are adopted?" I said "Yes," because that didn't leave room for more questions. If somebody asked, "Oh, did your mom go to Sierra Leone and meet your father?" I said "Yes." Lots of my friends had different interpretations of my background, because I just didn't want to go into discussion — not because I was ashamed, I just didn't think they were ready to hear that. Plus I wanted them to see me for what I was then — the kid who loved soccer, rapping, and hanging out with friends.

For me, I wanted people to see, to know, and to understand, when they learned my entire story, that there was an Ishmael before the war, during the war, and after the war. All of those things make me who I am, not just the "Ishmael during the war."

I felt that if I introduced myself the first time I met people through just "Ishmael in the war," that would be the only place they would stop, and they would not be able to go beyond that. So that's why I was reluctant.

I remember when the excerpt of the book came out in *The New York Times Magazine,* I got a lot of e-mails from friends from high school and

college, sort of saying that "we knew there was something you were hid-
ing all the time, you know."

I would laugh, because at some point in my experience, there are
always friends who find out one way or the other. I remember, for example, during my last year of high school, we were getting the yearbook
together and we took these pictures and put them in the yearbook, but
one of the areas of the yearbook that I couldn't participate in — which I
didn't say much about — was the baby picture side. Everyone wanted to
have a baby picture, but I could not provide one, and I did not explain
why. I just said I didn't have one. Some people — various people who
worked for the yearbook — their response was that "maybe you were just
an ugly baby, and you don't want to bring a baby picture."

Actually, I liked that explanation better, because I really didn't have
to explain. I realized that sometimes people don't appreciate how lucky
they are just to be able to have these sorts of paraphernalia about their
childhood that people might think is just useless, you know? But to
someone like me, it's something that I have nothing of at all.

Those kinds of moments were very difficult for me, but I always exercised my emotion privately. I am glad I wrote this book now so that I've
put it out there. I wrote this book as a way to just come out and explain
what had happened to me.

This book really came out of frustration, and it goes into the idea of
promoting respect for all human rights. One of the things that I began
to see is when any story is told from any part of the world without any
human context, it becomes hopeless. The media is bent on sensational-
izing stories without any human context.

When Sierra Leone began appearing on the news, it was spoken about
as if it had always had a civil war. Before our war, most people didn't know
about us, because we're a very small country. We became known to the
international community because of the civil war. For people whose first
encounter with Sierra Leone came through this sort of media portrayal
of this country, their perception became Sierra Leone equals civil war,
amputation, madness, and nothing more. They could not see the Sierra
Leone that existed before the war and what led to the destruction of the
traditions and the culture that were present before that.

It's a place where I grew up, where I went to school, learned

Shakespeare, where — because Sierra Leone is a former British colony — I learned a lot of American hip-hop.

When they used words such as *soliloquy* and *clandestine* in hip-hop lyrics, I would go to the dictionary — because English wasn't my first language — and look for the meaning of the word. I was interested because of the poetry in the words that were there, and the versatility in people's use of this English language that was quite foreign to me at that time. You will no longer find the usage of such words in most of the lyrics. Everyone seems to be rapping about their tires, how they're shiny, and whatever it is they're wearing, and other things.

[Sierra Leone was] also a place not only with Shakespeare, hip-hop, but also with a very strong community — a place where I grew up, where, as a child, I walked six, seven miles to my grandmother's village and no one would bother me. People would pull me over and cook food for me. There was storytelling in the evening where we sat around and adults told stories to young people. There was this strong sense of community, and all of these things disintegrated because of the war and other things.

When this country was spoken about, that context wasn't there. When people don't see that context, it begins to bring about a sense of hopelessness, because there is no presence of humanity within the telling of the story. Even during war, during times of chaos, people's humanity is still intact. Some might lose sight of it, but it's still there. And when we're unwilling to see that, when it's not present, it begins to show that these people's lives are not as valuable as ours who live over here, or that they are capable of that and we are not capable of it.

Once upon a time in Sierra Leone, we felt that way when war started in Liberia. Everyone said, "We can never be like that." But the human spirit is capable of losing itself completely. More important, it's capable of regaining that humanity. I wanted people to see that, not just how the destruction comes about.

So I think the idea of this respect for human rights really comes to the context in which stories are told; in other words, to understand that regardless of how people live their lives or what circumstances they are in, the sacrosanct nature of human life is the same. That's the biggest difficulty in understanding and respecting human rights right now, because I don't think as human beings we have gotten to that point where we truly believe that all life is valuable.

I'll tell you a story. I won't tell you the network or the reporter, but I was on the news. Before me, the reporter interviewed a soldier who had been in Afghanistan. Afterward I came and sat.

The first thing that the interviewer said to me was, "Well, this is the first time that I've had somebody sit in that chair who killed people."

And I said: "Oh, really? Well, you just had the soldier from Afghanistan who was sitting there. What do you think they are doing over there, cooking and hanging out?"

I was trying to lighten the mood a little bit just to get him to understand, but he still couldn't get it, and he said, "But that's a different kind of killing."

I said, "Oh, really?" And it hit me that there is still this idea that it is OK for some people to do certain things, and when certain lives are taken, it is OK.

I think that is the biggest problem we have now, because once we begin to understand that each person's life is absolutely valuable regardless of what our differences are, that would actually put us in a position of defending that life and caring for it when it's threatened. The way stories are told about other places, we're so removed from them. What I said earlier today to the young people with whom I had a dialogue is this idea that I always push to people — there is an absolute need for us to expose ourselves to the world more so than ever, not only to learn about places that have conflicts but places that don't yet have conflicts. When we do so, we get to learn about other people and see that they are as human as we are, that they still have the same human tendencies, desires, needs, and wants. When we reach that point, I think we are able to transform, to begin to change how we look at others, to begin to value their lives even if they don't have electricity or tap water. That doesn't mean they are not as human as we are.

For me, the way that Sierra Leone was spoken about lost the human context, and I wanted to put that human context in the story. More important, I wanted to speak about the strength of the human spirit, particularly children who are dragged into this war, how they fall into this madness, and how they come out of it. This is not often spoken about. What I wanted is for people not to ever think that children who are dragged into any kind of conflict are a lost generation, or to think that these children can never recover from their situation. I refuse to believe that, because if people had felt that way, I would not be standing in front of you.

I would have been left in a war. I would have been left in a place where I would not have been able to know anything. What I learned after I came out of this war is — when you're in a violent situation, a situation that only creates fear and distrust — what it does to the human spirit. It doesn't allow you to even have the luxury to know yourself, to know your own capacity to do something else. There's always fear, intimidation, which remove you from connecting with people, from seeing other people's humanity. That is very important to me.

I use the word *humanity* quite a lot because I think that's the common thing that we all have, regardless of where we are, what we look like, and things of that sort.

I really wanted to write this book as a way to show people that strength — the strength of the human spirit that is present in all of us. Some of us have seen that strength because life has thrown us these sorts of difficult times, but all of us have that strength within us. I want people to really believe that, particularly young people.

I wanted to write this book to show people that violence or war is not as romantic as people think it is. It's not as fascinating as people think it is. There is a fascination with it, because people are removed from the reality of it. People don't really know what it does to you when you are there. Being in this country almost ten years now, I've seen that. You see films, sometimes Hollywood films, where somebody is going to war and there is music in the background. There is rock and roll, and there is somebody during a gunfight who will pull out a phone and call his wife or girlfriend to tell her he loves her. These are Hollywood realities of what war is like.

The reality of war? There is no background music, first of all. Second, you don't have the luxury to call your girlfriend or your wife. You don't have the luxury to even love yourself. During war, you dehumanize other people in order to take their life, but what no one wants to believe — which is true — is that when you dehumanize somebody, when you hate somebody severely, even without war, what it does in reverse: you hate yourself and you dehumanize yourself. It takes a lot of undoing too.

But people don't want to believe these things. These are the truths that are very difficult to come to terms with, because what it means is that if we believe completely that when we engage in war, when we kill other people, it does something to us, regardless of what the reason is for that war, then we would not have a case for war. We would not have people joining armies to fight, because they would know that it actually torments you. People don't want to talk about that, because that actually goes against what we've come to believe is the only way to solve our problems. But it's not.

I learned something very interesting, perhaps even life-changing, that I will share with you. When I was in the war, I lost my immediate family — my mother, father, and two brothers were killed. I became the only survivor of my family. When I was dragged into the war, one of the motivating things about it was the chance to avenge the death of my family. With the drugs, the constant violence, everything, I came to believe that was true.

I was removed from the war, and I began to make friends with kids who were in the RUF[1] or other groups that fought in the war. They were told the same rhetoric. They were told that we (the enemy) were responsible for what had happened to them and that we didn't deserve to live. Everyone had the same rhetoric but a different enemy. This created a cycle of violence, and with this sort of hate, we took other peoples' lives, other people who had *nothing* to do with what happened to us. The people who survived those massacres had more reason to be part of this madness, and so we were creating an escalating cycle of violence.

When I was removed from the war and I learned this reality, it was difficult for me to handle — to understand that we perpetuated this thing when we thought that we were doing something to prevent it, because we were so lost in it. I realized that revenge doesn't do anything to anyone at all. It doesn't pay. It doesn't help us stop or understand why a place where your neighbor once fed you, bathed you, and clothed you became your enemy. With revenge, you never have the time to sit down and understand. That only comes about through forgiveness.

Forgiveness is also a word that people throw around quite a lot. It is not easy. It is absolutely difficult. But I have come to learn that beneficial things are always difficult. Everything that is easy is usually not very good for us to do.

When you forgive somebody, it allows you to understand the situation. It allows you to transform it positively so that people can learn from it. Forgiveness is not just saying, "I forgive you, I forgive you"; it is also a process with a practical aspect.

In Sierra Leone, there was a Truth and Reconciliation Commission after the war ended, and through it people forgave one another, but if you forgive somebody for burning your entire village and two years later your village is still burned, you're going to be upset. It's a natural human reaction. Forgiveness must come with some sort of development, some practical thing in people's lives. It's not enough just to say, "I forgive you, I forgive you."

I grew up in a society — this is not spoken about much — where, before the war, punishment was based on rehabilitation instead of retaliation. When I was growing up, if somebody wronged another person in the community, the punishment was to hang out and help that person with his or her farm. Some people might think that's ridiculous, but when you spend a week or so working on somebody's farm, hanging out, eating from the same plate, resting together, and going to the river together, you repair the relationship that was damaged. That was the idea of rehabilitation as opposed to punitive measures. Punitive measures do not provide an understanding of how to prevent the reoccurrence of some injury. We throw somebody in jail, we do something to them, and that's the end of that. We don't really understand what happened. How can we prevent that, how can we see traces of humanity in other people so that we can prevent that kind of injury? For me, it is essential to promote and respect human rights and respect everyone's life. We need to be able not only to see people's humanity but to learn to forgive and more important to learn to expose ourselves to the world and learn about other people's lives, other people's cultures beyond our environment, beyond New York City, beyond the United States. When we do so, I believe it will be difficult to make a case for war.

This is why I'm amazed when I go to certain conferences where there are kids from Brazil, from Iraq, from Afghanistan, and they all sit a room and talk. Sometimes people say: "Well, what would that do? They're not going to get anything out of it."

Perhaps nothing comes of it immediately, but what is important is that people make friends from another part of the world. Ten, fifteen years from now, those kids in that room may become a leader in Afghanistan or Iraq or the United States. All of them are less likely to engage in war because they know someone in that country. They can pick up the phone and call and say, "Hey, man, what are you doing?"

I think the world hasn't been like that. There's been a disassociation. We say: "They are like that but we are not, so therefore they are bad. They are wrong, we are right. They are this; we are that." We have lost sight of what's really important, which is the idea there's so much that we have in common. The little differences that we have don't mean much at all, but oftentimes that's what is amplified.

Another thing that I've come to realize is that if you really look at our world right now, there are very few people who really disrupt the state of our world. Very few! The rest of us are good, and we say we're good, but we don't do much to actually show that goodness. The few people who disrupt our world are so committed that they actually have been able to disrupt our world. The rest of us who are good are not as committed as they are. If we are as committed as they are, we can outdo them.

So much is going on around the world — it's overwhelming when you turn on the television, when you read the news. People sometimes feel: "There's nothing I can do. What would my contribution do, the problem is so big?" If everyone felt that way, no problem would ever be fixed. If everyone felt that way, I wouldn't be standing in front of you. If everyone thought: "Oh, these kids who are dragged into this war, what can I do? It's sad, but what can I do?"

But there are people who are willing to say, "All right, we can do our part, change other people's lives." Each one of us, our contribution is absolutely valuable and important. But I want it to come from a genuine and compassionate place in you, a human place in you. I don't want people to just feel that it's enough to donate, say, five dollars to some charity. I want you to be invested in what that money is going to do, to take time to learn about where that money is going. You learn about other people's lives. You include them into your life.

Everyone always asks me why my book has reached so many people, why people react to it so strongly? I don't have the answers, but one thing I know is that I believe it tapped into our common humanity. When people read this book, they see themselves in it. They see traces of their children, they see traces of themselves. I grew up listening in the days of Run DMC, MC Hammer. These are things that connect us, through music, through this shared culture, this shared humanity. That's what has been effective about the book. For the first time, it wasn't just a book that says, "another madhouse in Africa, another mad country in the African continent."

Throughout colonialism and even today, there's very little known about contemporary Africa, so, there are many misperceptions of this place. Again, it goes to why I'm proposing to people to learn about these places. Perhaps the last time some read anything about Africa was Chinua Achebe's *Things Fall Apart*. It's a very good book, but that period no longer exists in Africa. Or perhaps some people saw National Geographic's episodes, usually where they have some African with no shirt on and navigating a charred landscape. I've actually never met those Africans. I don't know where they found them for these kinds of shows.

But these are the kinds of understanding that people have of Africa. Images that are so remote to the point that they don't see that people who live in these places are very connected to the world. Oftentimes I am asked questions like: "Oh, how do you know so much about hip-hop? You're from Africa." My response to them is always: "Africa is on this planet. It's not on some other planet."

We are much closer than people are willing to believe. What happens in Africa can affect people here as well. In Sierra Leone or Uganda or the Congo or Sri Lanka or wherever these problems are — there are external factors involved. For example, in Sierra Leone, we don't have any guns, but during the war we had all kinds of guns. People quickly put the blame on Russia and China, but those are not the only places the guns are coming from.

Guns are coming even from the United States. People don't want to believe that. You know, I'm not telling you some secondhand research paper. I was there. We had M-16s, which are primarily U.S. assault rifles. They are not coming from anywhere else. We had G3s, German rifles. Guns are coming from everywhere.

Let's take a scenario in Sierra Leone or in the Congo during the days of Mobuto. When these leaders start being corrupt, where do they keep their money? Abroad, right? They steal everything from the nation and ruin the nation's revenue. Meanwhile, people are poor, desperate, destitute, and demoralized. When they get to that point, you can sell anything to them. They will believe anything, because they want to blame somebody for what happened to them. Imagine if this was a world where people were willing to say, "We cannot keep that money in the bank." If a leader from one of these countries has thirty or forty billion dollars — it's not rocket science; you know it's not their money. Unless you're doing some seriously interesting business, you cannot make that much money by yourself as a leader and rule a country as well. Imagine if banks like the Suisse Bank had blocked the putting of money into these banks. Those leaders would not be able to embezzle funds, because if you steal thirty billion dollars in Sierra Leone and have it at your house, people will pay you a visit and it will not be a very good one.

But people have come to believe that their lives are not important to us, that we don't care, that what happens to them doesn't affect us; eventually it affects all of us. The world is so intertwined and small now that we cannot ignore problems that are happening just outside of our borders. My appeal to you is that, whatever issue you're passionate about, take time to learn about it and also try to learn about other people's lives elsewhere. Also, appreciate what you have.

I don't want people to feel bad about what they have, but rather to appreciate it because it helps them to know that there are people who are worse off. When I came here, I started school at a place that had desks, that had books and textbooks that could be checked out. That was enough reason for me to be in school every day, because I was coming from a place where people don't have those luxuries. I just want people to really appreciate what they have and take advantage of their situation and oftentimes stop and think about what they can do to help other people.

So with that, I am going to read a little bit about how this war came into my life. My older brother, Junior, and a friend, Talloi, had gone to a talent show — we were into American hip-hop — when the war came to our town, Mogbwemo. We tried to go back and find our family and this is when we began to see how this landscape changed tremendously, to the point that we could feel even nature itself was afraid of what was unfolding.

I grew up in the countryside. I only came to the capital because of the war. One of the strangest things that happened in Sierra Leone is that, in the morning, there will be birds singing and animals making different sounds to signal different times during the day. When the war came, all of that ceased. It quieted. It felt as though even nature, even the animals, were afraid that something different was happening on this landscape. What I'm describing is sort of how you can see the land begin to change, how people related to one another. A place where once young people would not raise their voice to adults became a place where those same young people were forced to kill those adults. It changed the dynamics of how people related to one another, tremendously.

From *A Long Way Gone: Memoirs of a Boy Soldier* (pp. 11–12):

> Junior, Talloi, and I jumped into a canoe and sadly waved to our friends as the canoe pulled away from the shores of Matru Jong. As we landed on the other side of the river, more and more people were arriving in haste. We started walking, and a woman carrying her flip-flops on her head spoke without looking at us: "Too much blood has been spilled where you are going. Even the good spirits have fled from that place." She walked past us. In the bushes along the river, the strained voices of women cried out, "*Nguwor gbor mu ma oo,*" God help us, and screamed the names of their children. "Yusufu, Jabu, Foday …" We saw children walking by themselves, shirtless, in their underwear, following the crowd. "*Nya nje oo, nya keke oo,*" my mother, my father, the children were crying. There were also dogs running in between the crowds of people, who were still running, even though far away from harm. The dogs sniffed the air, looking for their owners. My veins tightened.
>
> We had walked six miles and were now at Kabati, Grandmother's village. It was deserted. All that was left were footprints in the sand leading toward the dense forest that spread out beyond the village.

As evening approached, people started arriving from the mining area. Their whispers, the cries of little children seeking lost parents and tired of walking, and the wails of hungry babies replaced the evening songs of crickets and birds. We sat on Grandmother's verandah, waiting and listening.

"Do you guys think it is a good idea to go back to Mogbwemo?" Junior asked. But before either of us had a chance to answer, a Volkswagen roared in the distance and all the people walking on the road ran into the nearby bushes. We ran, too, but didn't go that far. My heart pounded and my breathing intensified. The vehicle stopped in front of my grandmother's house, and from where we lay we could see that whoever was inside the car was not armed. As we, and others, emerged from the bushes, we saw a man run from the driver's seat to the sidewalk, where he vomited blood. His arm was bleeding. When he stopped vomiting, he began to cry. It was the first time I had seen a grown man cry like a child, and I felt a sting in my heart.

A woman put her arms around the man and begged him to stand up. He got to his feet and walked toward the van. When he opened the door opposite the driver's, a woman who was leaning against it fell to the ground. Blood was coming out of her ears. People covered the eyes of their children.

In the back of the van were three more dead bodies: two girls and a boy, and their blood was all over the seats and the ceiling of the van. I wanted to move away from what I was seeing, but couldn't. My feet went numb and my entire body froze. Later we learned that the man had tried to escape with his family and the rebels had shot at his vehicle, killing all his family. The only thing that consoled him, for a few seconds at least, was when the woman who had embraced him, and now cried with him, told him that at least he would have the chance to bury them. He would always know where they were laid to rest, she said. She seemed to know a little more about war than the rest of us....

The last casualty that we saw that evening was a woman who carried her baby on her back. Blood was running down her dress and dripping behind her, making a trail. Her child had been shot dead as she ran for her life. Luckily for her, the bullet didn't go through the baby's body. When she stopped at where we stood, she sat on the ground and removed her child. It was a girl, and her eyes were still open with an interrupted innocent smile on her face. The bullets could be seen sticking out just a little bit in the baby's body and she was swelling. The mother clung to her child and rocked her. She was in too much pain and shock to shed tears.

I wanted this story to bring you to see what was changing in this landscape and how that was for a child, for a young person who was twelve years old. There was no one to explain what was happening, the uncertainty and the difficulty of seeing these things was in fact traumatizing. This was all before I was even dragged to fight in the war. Our lives went from thinking we had a future to wondering how we would survive the next minute? And if we did survive, can we survive the next minute? That became the extent of how far we could think of our lives.

When you are in that position, you lose sight of all things. Then, when you are dragged into an army, it only gets worse. At some point when I was in the war, I lost even the ability to exhibit any human emotion at all, because feeling remorse or crying if a friend was killed was not accepted. As time goes on, we became hardened and could not react emotionally.

After the war, each of us had to undo all of these things. I had to learn even how to sleep. When I saw [the movie] *Blood Diamond* — good movie, it raised a lot of awareness — one of the things that upset me was how it made it seem that recovering from war is easy. A lot of people believe in quick fixes; that you can remove the child from the war and shake him and say, "You are a good child," and the child cries and is fine. That's how the movie paints it.

When I came from the war, however, it took me eight months just to learn how to sleep, how to want to think back before the war, and so on. Why the picture of a quick fix is dangerous is because, when people see films like *Blood Diamond* and believe that recovery is easy, then a child who doesn't recover within a month or two is considered finished, and that creates a bigger problem.

Even during the times that I described to you right now, I saw how remarkable the human spirit is, and how people are able to find hope in hopelessness itself. When we were running from the war, what gave us strength? It was hope. Hope is a form of strength. We found a rotten orange one day, and we ate it. We thought, maybe tomorrow we will find one that's not rotten, and that's what kept us alive for the next day. If we found some water and drank it, or we found some clothes in a village where people had run away and wore them — we would think, maybe tomorrow things will change.

In Sierra Leone, I believe hope is one of the strongest things that people have, that's the resilience of my country. People are very hopeful. During the war, people would say: "Oh, it will end tomorrow," or "It will end next week." Such thoughts might have been a lie to some people, but they saved people's lives.

When I was running from the war, one of my friends died along the way. I strongly believe that, apart from malnourishment and things like that, he lost the strength to carry on. He lost hope. He felt there was no reason to go on, because we had all lost our families and what was the point? That made him weak, and so he gave in. Hope itself is a form of strength.

I was at New York University at a talk on Africa. Every speaker talked about how bad it was in Africa. I was sitting there getting frustrated and thinking to myself that if I weren't from Sierra Leone or West Africa, I would think Africa is finished. It's so hopeless, no one lives there, nothing can be done about it. But Africa is still there, you know.

So, I was sitting there, and I raised my hand and asked, "Did anyone at least have a nice flight to Africa?"

Several speakers immediately talked about good meetings they had with people there.

"Well, why don't you speak about that?" I asked. "Not only the bad?" I'm not saying that there aren't bad things happening there. There are. But there are also good things. People continue to live there.

The reason I am able to live with the memories of the war is because of the foundation of my childhood in Africa, the strength that I have within me. These things are not spoken about. Not talking about the good things removes us from that humanity; it prevents us from understanding the strength that is there. It's not because of hopelessness that people still live there.

When I went back home in 2006, I went with some American

rappers. A friend of mine, Raquel Cepeda, was making a film called *Bling the Planet Rock,* taking American rappers to Sierra Leone to learn about what had happened there.

When we arrived, we went to get phones for everyone. American phones don't work abroad, because they are locked. A kid on the street says to me, "Sam" — which is like saying "Yo, man" in Krio. He says, "Let me see your phone." So I give him my phone, and he unlocks it. He's a kid on the street, but he knows how to open it. Then he says, "Well, now that you know I can unlock your phone, I can unlock all the other eight that you have for your friends at this price."

Usually prices can be negotiated, but I could not negotiate this particular price, because I was thinking to myself: "Now, here is this kid, he doesn't even have a phone of his own, but he has technology and business skills. But he can only use them to survive, because that's his only choice. He is in touch with the world, but the world is not in touch with him at all, because it's general opinion that there is nothing he can do beyond that. If that same energy is refocused, that intelligence is refocused, that kid can do other things with his life."

These are the kinds of stories that are not newsworthy. No one would report about that, because that doesn't paint the picture they expect to see. Even after coming as far as I have, people are always asking me about the news. People think that living with the memories of war, living with trauma, means to carry the burden as opposed to transforming it positively, as opposed to turning those experiences into instructional tools.

That's the understanding. People feel that's the only way you can live with this sort of experience. I will never forget what happened in the war, and there are so many tendencies I live with on a daily basis because of it. But I transform them, sometimes in funny ways.

For example, I have insomnia. I don't sleep very well because of the war. Now I could think that's a hardship, but I don't. When I was a student — particularly in college — this was an advantage, having insomnia.

Because I could not sleep, I did my work ahead of time. I wrote this book when I was in college.

I try to show people that there are ways to transform. When it becomes a burden, it doesn't help anyone at all; it doesn't even help you. There's a way to transform experiences so they are not a burden, and people should learn to understand that and see that. That's what I try to show people.

The strength that I gained as a child in Sierra Leone really stays with me and in my writing. What I do comes from that.

There was a strong oral tradition in my culture and that plays a lot with my writing. I grew up in a village, and every evening I went to see my grandmother. We sat around the fire and the adults would tell stories to the young people. One thing about storytelling is that it facilitates active listening. When you are told a story orally, you are not taking notes. You have to remember, you have to pay attention to internalize the information. The way the adults tested that was, two, three, four days later, they would randomly call upon a younger person in the audience to retell a story we'd been told.

If you weren't listening, you could not tell the story. And when you grow up in a very small village, you don't want to be known as the child who doesn't listen. That's bad news for you. So you listen carefully, and when you start retelling the story, the adults, they paid attention.

These stories had to do with moral and ethical standards of the community: what it means to live in a community, histories of certain towns and villages, histories of families and individuals, and so on.

Those stories you could not change at all. When you were telling one of these stories, the adults paid attention. When you added or removed anything from the story, you were immediately smacked in front of everyone. They were not punishing you, just reminding you that when you destroy the backbone of a story, you destroy the purpose and the functionality of the story.

There are a few stories that have the leeway to be changed, but not all of them. As a kid growing up, my early sense of narrative was already there before I even knew I wanted to write. When I started writing, I also realized the beauty, not only of my culture — the community and things like that — but also the language. As a kid, I'd come to believe that the English language was the best possible thing I could know. Coming from a former British colony, my parents even put that in my head — "English is the best language. Learn it." — to the point that our own languages were considered vernacular. When we spoke anything other than English in school, we were disciplined for it.

As I was writing, I realized that when I wanted to translate conversations from Mende, Krio, Temne, or any of the languages in Sierra Leone, I struggled to find an English equivalent, and that struggle is what made this book what it is. For example, in Sierra Leone, particularly in my tribe, Mende, a certain phrase might be translated into English as "Night came suddenly." But in Mende, the actual phrase is, literally translated, "The sky rolled over and changed its sides." That's how you say, "Night came suddenly."

It's in my culture, the language and the beauty of it. There's a belief that there's power in language, that it can be used to bring people closer to something or to actually touch people deeply.

People often speak in parables, especially the older folks, so if you were to go to some part of my country and someone says to you, "My dog sleeps in the cooking area," you might think we have a dog problem. Let's feed the dogs, let's put a door to the kitchen and many other interpretations. But that's not what it means. When somebody says, "My dog sleeps in the cooking area," it means that the family is hungry. If they were cooking every day, the ashes in the cooking area would always be warm. But if you don't cook for weeks, the ashes are cold, so the dog can actually lay there. That's the interpretation.

So when I was writing, I began to realize that someone can genuinely care about this culture and want to help people, but without that cultural understanding that person can misinterpret so many things and bring about help that is not necessary. This is why I'm saying it's important to expose yourself to the world.

I was at a conference not so long ago — the American Psychiatric Association, a wonderful conference. People go sometimes who deal with mental health issues of children coming from this war. In my culture, children don't look at adults when they are talking to them. Children don't raise their heads. It's a sign of respect. That was part of my culture. Children from that culture, even if they have been through a war and have recovered, they would still have that demeanor. For a psychologist or anyone coming from the outside who doesn't know that, they might think a child who walks around not looking adults is the most disturbed, let's give him more medicine. And that could actually devastate the life of the child. This is true. Cultural understanding is absolutely important.

There is an idea that has been going around, which I think comes from a genuine place — this idea of one computer per child. People want to give computers so that people are connected to the world. From the outside it seems nice, right?

But actually, for some communities and cultures, it's not good. That's a Western standard. If you give every child a computer in a place where community is central to how people function, you isolate everyone. Everyone all of a sudden feels that "Oh, with my computer, I don't need anyone anymore. I can go on the Internet."

If, instead, you give three or four computers and put them at a village center, everyone congregates around that and learns how to use the computer. There is a transfer of knowledge within the community. That's actually much more effective.

Last, I was in Cameroon in the north, and the north is very remote. Some people think, "Oh, we should have running water in every house." It sounds like a good idea, but it's not. That's because, in some of these places, women don't have much freedom. The only time these women have the freedom to be in the domain of only women is when they go to the water well to fetch water. That's when they can talk to one another, gossip about their husbands, and so on. This is quite healthy. If, instead, you give each house a tap with running water, they no longer have that freedom.

The only way we're going to understand one another, value one another's lives, one another's cultures, is to expose ourselves to the world more. And once we do so, we understand the value of each human life. That's how we can gain that respect for humanity and for human rights as well.

May 12, 2008
SGI-USA New York Culture of Peace Resource Center

NOTE:

1   RUF: Revolutionary United Front was a rebel army in Sierra Leone from 1991 to 2002 before evolving into a political party that existed until 2007. It was initially popular with Sierra Leoneans but eventually developed an international reputation for cruelty and crimes against humanity.

Child Rights and the Culture of Peace

Kimmie Weeks
Child Rights Activist

Kimmie Weeks has worked to alleviate poverty and human suffering in Africa and around the world since the age of fourteen. He was born in Liberia, West Africa, in 1981. When he was nine years old, he came face to face with civil war, human suffering, and death. These experiences encouraged Weeks to try to make a difference, working to ensure a world where all children have access to food, medicine, and shelter. He has pursued that vision ever since. Weeks has formed partnerships and led organizations that have provided education for thousands of students in West Africa and lobbied for the disarmament of more than twenty thousand child soldiers. The Liberian government attempted to assassinate him for a report he issued on its involvement in the training of child soldiers.

Weeks fled Liberia at seventeen and was granted political asylum in the United States. His focus is empowering people, providing new opportunities, creating strategic development partnerships with Africa and the West, and using technology to link Africa with the rest of the world. He is featured in the book *Peace in Our Lifetime* alongside Nelson Mandela, Gandhi, and Martin Luther King Jr. His passion for his mission is found in his unique situation, which gives him the ability and opportunity to connect children in need to those young people who have the potential to help.

> Kimmie Weeks speaks compellingly of many topics included in the eight action areas in the 1999 United Nations Declaration and Programme of Action on a Culture of Peace, especially the seventh: Supporting participatory communication and the free flow of information and knowledge. He says: "Let's see ourselves as equals moving forward—that helping Africa is about providing the tools, the fertilizer, and relying on the know-how of the people who for generations were able to feed themselves. Why can's we listen to the old ladies who didn't go to Harvard or Princeton, but know their reality better than any PhD holder from an Ivy League school does? *They* know it."

I'm thankful for many things. One is the opportunity to be involved in work that changes the lives of so many people. I hope that people will leave this room tonight feeling that they want to do more. Most people who attend speeches like this are already engaged and conscious in some way. But the key is for everyone to believe that they can do more than they're doing now and for each and every person to get others engaged.

I've come to talk about extreme poverty in Africa — the type of poverty that kills; that strangles; that forces mothers to watch as their children die from hunger; that forces families to watch as their children and relatives die from diseases that could have been cured for a few cents.

Resources Versus Will

We live in a very unfortunate world. At no point in history have we had the resources, the know-how and the technology to end world poverty that we have now. But the unfortunate truth is that, in this same world, at no point in history have there been so many people suffering and in pain around the globe. How do we reconcile that? On one hand, we've got the resources and the know-how but, on the other, we have the greatest number of people ever living with and dying from hunger.

I have a photo that was taken in East Africa. It shows a young boy whose mother had died from starvation. The baby, nearly dead from starvation himself, is struggling to crawl away from his mother's body. And in the distance, a vulture is waiting for this child to die so that it can take his body. This happened a few years ago, not in the Middle Ages, not in prehistoric times. It was about ten years ago.

It is happening today: Every single day, more than thirty thousand children around the world die from preventable causes; thirty thousand children die from diseases that the world has cures for; thirty thousand children die because they don't have food to eat.

Civil War in Liberia

I remember my own situation. I was a little guy in 1989. Before the First Liberian Civil War[1] started, we never thought we'd undergo such circumstances — never imagined that we would live in extreme poverty, when we wouldn't have food to eat. When she was young, my mom came here to New York to study at the Fashion Institute of Technology. She had mapped out her life, never imagining that the day would come when she would watch her son have no food to eat and there would be absolutely nothing she could do about it. But that day came in 1989, when civil war started in Liberia.

I remember when Charles Taylor[2] declared war in 1989. He said that, when this war happened, things would get better for everybody. People saw it as a grand revolution. I remember people went out in the streets, dancing and celebrating. I was nine years old. I didn't understand the politics, but I didn't have to go to school that day so I went out dancing and singing too. It was good times.

Then we began to see the images of war coming toward us. Before this I had only seen images of poverty as we watched the Ethiopian famine in the 1980s. As a kid, that was strange to me. I often said to my mom: "How is it possible that there are kids in the world who don't have food to eat? Why are flies sitting on those kids?" It just seemed so far away.

Of course my mom would say: "Oh, Maurice! Eat your food." But then the war came. Suddenly it went from being far away to being on our doorsteps. We watched as the rebels advanced. They were coming closer to us and we feared that the destruction would hit our home. Eventually it did. I remember when it came. There was constant gunfire, fighting, shooting, and missiles falling. My mom and I had to lay down on the floor of our house, fearing that, at any moment, a bullet would fly through one of the windows or a missile would fall on the house. We were very afraid.

This went on for several days until the rebels finally took over our home. They had been going from house to house, knocking on doors and forcing people out of their homes. They came to our house and put us out. We weren't allowed to take anything but the clothing we were wearing. We got on a national highway and I remember, as far as the eye could see, there were thousands of people walking to find new homes. At this point, I was the laziest bum in the world. I had never walked a day in my life, so I was crying just that we were forced to walk.

Life and Death as a Refugee

We began to see shocking things firsthand; things that we never thought we would see; things that my mom had never even let me watch on TV. People were being killed right before us, women being raped. For the first time, I saw children my own age, ten or twelve years old, holding, not the rubber guns and water guns we used to play with, but real guns; fighting and killing. It was a shocking thing to see.

In Liberia, children were brought up to respect adults. It was as if the entire society had transformed — now young children were holding guns and committing atrocities against adults. One image I'll never forget was a mother who had been killed, her body left on the wayside. Her baby, probably three or four years old, was just sitting by his mother, crying. People were passing by; nobody was stopping to help. I will never forget that.

We walked the entire day and came to the Fendell Campus of Liberia University. It was originally built for about four thousand students. Now, almost the entire population of the capital had been forced to find refuge there. By the time we arrived, most of the classrooms were filled to overflowing. People started to lie down on the sidewalks. We had been walking around for a long time when someone from one of the rooms called out to us and said, "If it's only the two of you, come in." We walked into a small classroom. There were about sixteen families there. My mom spread out a cloth between two of them. This was to be our home for the next six months.

The first night there our parents said to us: "Don't worry. We live in a caring world. We live in a global community. Liberia was a founding member of the United Nations. There will be airlifts for us; there will be a D-Day for Liberia; U.N. peacekeepers will come and rescue us." That was the hope they had for us. But in a few days that hope disappeared. The people who had brought food to us started to run out of it. That's when the real suffering kicked in.

First, newborn babies started to die from starvation. Imagine for a moment that you're a parent. You spend your entire life working to feed your family. Now, because of a war you have nothing to do with, you watch your children die from hunger and there is absolutely nothing you can do about it — nothing.

My mom and I started to go with the other people in the camp to the woods to find roots and leaves, things that people never thought they would be eating. The water we drank looked discolored at times and smelled bad, but it was all that we had. So, we drank it. People started to get sick from cholera, water-borne illnesses. It reached a point where so many people were dying that they stopped burying them. The bodies began to pile up. Every evening we came out and looked in the distance where the bodies were piling up.

Rising From the Dead

I became very sick. I stopped moving. I was just lying on the floor instead of waking up and seeing my mother and her smiling, reassuring face. I started to think I would be a chef, because all I could think about was food. Food, food, food; in my mind, I was making food all over the place. McDonald's would have nothing on me. All we could hope for was tomorrow, just living to see the next day. It wasn't living to see five years or ten years; it was just *praying* that we would see the next day.

I had been sick for many days and people were concerned that I hadn't woken up for a long time. Everybody came to my mom, ask- ing: "Is he OK? What's going on with Kimmie?" She kept saying: "Oh, he's fine. Everything's OK." Finally people stopped believing her. Two of the men held my mom while another person felt my pulse. This per- son wasn't a medical doctor, but he said I had died. They immediately wrapped me up in the cloth we had been lying on, took my body, threw me away on one of the heaps of bodies, and left me there.

When they came back, they let my mom go. People thought she had gone crazy because she went from heap to heap, pile to pile, searching for hours among the dead bodies to find me.

All I can remember from this experience is feeling a violent shak- ing on my body and waking up to see the pain and grief on my mom's face — seeing her crying for the first time. It was the only time she cried during the entire war. I had no idea that I was laying on a pile of bodies. It was just this sense of 'What is going on that my mom's crying?' Then they took me inside. That was after we had been in the camp for just a month. We stayed there for a total of six months. Over the course of the civil war, more than two hundred thousand people — about 10 percent of the population of Liberia — died, mostly from hunger and disease — two hundred thousand people.

A man, his wife, and their six children had come to the camp with us. By the time we left the camp, they had lost every single one of their children. Only the man and his wife were left alive.

Small Gestures

I remember the first time that we got food and healthcare in the camp. There was a UNICEF person distributing food. I remember her because we were supposed to get just one scoop of porridge and one biscuit. She must have thought that this kid was about to go. She said, "I'm going to give you an extra scoop." She did and she gave me an extra biscuit too. It was a very small gesture. She probably does not remember the kid she gave an extra scoop to. But I've never forgotten that small gesture and I can remember that woman's face.

I tell you this because it is the small gestures that matter to the people we extend them to — the things we think people don't pay attention to, the things we think have no impact whatsoever. Many people refuse to take action because they feel that what they can do is so small and insignificant, that it's not worth the time. Let the person on the other end of it be the judge of that and just do.

When I left, I thought that only we in Liberia were suffering. Imagine my shock when I left Liberia and had the opportunity to come to the United States and started to see suffering and pain on a global level — across Africa, across the world — the millions of people without access to healthcare. When I talk about healthcare, I'm not talking about the absence of health insurance. I'm talking about children and families who will get sick and who, even if they have the money, don't have a doctor to go to.

Doctors and Dollars

In parts of Africa, most children will become sick. They will wake up in the morning and walk an entire day to get to a doctor at the nearest clinic. They will stand in a long line with people who have come from villages very far away. After they arrive, they will wait the rest of the day until it's finally their turn to see the doctor. They may be told that the doctor has seen enough people for today, to go home and come back. They will have to walk all the way back home and return the next day or the day after.

Imagine the disappointment, after finally getting to see the doctor, of being told: "You have malaria, but we don't have the medicine that will cure you. Go home and pray." That is the reality for millions of people. Most of the drugs that are missing from the hospitals are drugs that sell for just a few dollars. But there is no willpower to provide these drugs to the world's poorest people.

As we drove across Uganda, we saw entire villages and towns that were simply empty, just empty. When we asked what had happened, we were told that the entire populations of these villages had died from AIDS — entire villages empty because every single person had died from AIDS. If they weren't empty, you would see villages of only children. It was like a bad movie — children all over and no adults. It reached a point that the United Nations had to create the new phrase "child-led households." It's hard to imagine that we have officially accepted that there is something called a child-led household, but this is the reality for millions of kids who are orphaned because of AIDS.

As we walked through Kroo Bay, one of the poorest communities in Freetown, Sierra Leone, we saw poverty on unimaginable levels. Children with cholera simply lied down on the ground to die; their parents couldn't take them to a hospital. There was hunger throughout the camp. It's a shantytown and with an open sewer running through it. Dirt, debris, and trash are on both sides of the waterway. It's clear that the water is unsafe, but upstream, children were bathing in it and downstream a woman is doing her laundry. It was the same water that people had to drink from. This is extreme poverty. None of the people in Kroo Bay want their children bathing in filth, none want to wash their laundry in filthy water, but they simply have no other option.

We had been to many poor countries and I had seen children begging before, but never had we seen the hundreds of babies that we saw begging on the streets of Kampala in Uganda. Their parents had left them out for maximum sympathy. Some of them could barely walk but they were out there begging. We met a woman in another slum area living in a very small room, maybe ten feet by fifteen feet with several families living there. She sits in her own spot; the woman behind her — that's her spot. People are packed together like sardines. Up above her head hangs the plastic bag that contains all her worldly possessions. You know you are facing extreme poverty when everything you own in the world can fit into one plastic bag.

This woman was sick and had been for weeks, but she simply couldn't get to a hospital. Here's a rather disturbing picture: When we got to Camp Kasenyi, we saw so many sick children. We asked for a list of the forty sickest children to take to the hospital the next day. They were dying from cholera and malaria, just lying down and dying. The next day we found that one of the babies on the list had died during the night. Her parents insisted that we take her picture to show the world that their child had died.

What shocked me was these families couldn't go to the hospital because they couldn't afford it. But when we took the kids to the hospital, none of their treatments was more than twenty dollars. The children were dying while their treatments cost less than twenty dollars each. This should be outrageous.

In Spite of Everything: Hope

On the flip side of all this, I see tremendous hope for Africa. Once I was giving one of these talks and someone said, "Geez, man, you just managed to make us all feel guilty." I said: "Good! I want to come to your bedroom and make you feel guilty some more!" But there's really no need for us to go home feeling guilty. There's reason for us to go away feeling hopeful.

The reason I feel hopeful isn't because I read Jeffrey Sachs or another economist who says there's a possibility for ending world poverty. My hope comes from going to these very poor communities, which you would assume to have the highest suicide rates. But I look in the faces of the children and they're still smiling and playing. I see mothers who have gone through extreme circumstances, who watched their children die and don't know where the next meal is coming from saying, "I know there's a better tomorrow and I'm going to live to see that better tomorrow." I see young men and young women who have no hope for employment, who still say,

"I'm going to keep trying and whatever I can do to better myself, I will do it."

Homegrown Ingenuity

In Sierra Leone, we opened a skills training center for the women in Kroo Bay, the community I mentioned earlier. Women flooded into the center; all of them had so much hope for the future. People of twenty-five, who had never been to school in their life, were still saying: "I dream of being a doctor so I can help my people. I dream of being an engineer." They didn't know where they would go to school, but their dream was still alive.

I see so much ingenuity when I travel across the continent, people making ends meet with very meager resources. In Sierra Leone, we met a young man who had very little formal training and had never been to school. But, from scraps, this guy had developed a rice cooker that could be started with a call from a cell phone; when the rice was done it would send a text message back saying that the rice had finished cooking.

There is so much ingenuity within the continent and I truly believe that this is the hope for Africa. A part of the problem so far is that many feel that the solution for Africa should be made in New York and transferred to Africa. I think this is where we have failed. People also believe that the key for Africa is simply to provide food aid. This is another failure to understand the true needs of the continent.

Someone once said to me, "Africans like to get free food; that's why they're always going to have wars." And I said, "Ooh, thank goodness I'm a peace activist or else I would be something else!"

Nothing could be further from the truth. African people are very proud of their heritage and culture. Nothing hurts a family more than having to stand on a relief line for food. I know this because after the First Liberian Civil War, it was true that the first few times we got relief food everybody was happy. But then several months passed and all we got was food aid. Then a year, two years passed, and we were still getting food aid.

Everybody started to say: "When are they going to give us tools to go back and farm? When are they going to give us seeds to go back and grow our own food?" And that didn't happen. People wanted to work for

themselves. This is what needs to change for Africa. We need to transform aid from dumping food to entering a partnership with the people
in Africa. Let's see ourselves as equals moving forward — that helping Africa is about providing the tools, the fertilizer, and relying on the
know-how of the people who for generations were able to feed themselves. Why can't we listen to the old ladies who didn't go to Harvard or
Princeton, but know their reality better than any PhD holder from an
Ivy League school does? *They* know it.

These are the people we should be turning to for the solutions to
the problems. Until that happens we cannot change the world. We have
opened centers across Africa where women make products. It's incredible. We just open the centers and find the money to run them, but
the women themselves teach one another and come up with the ideas
for these products. There was never a day that I went to a center and
said, "Why don't you create this bag or that necklace?" It is completely
internal and they've created amazing, beautiful products. They've made
necklaces and bags from recycled glass that they collected and bags from
grass and rice straws that people would have discarded. They've made
incredible products and they didn't need a PhD to tell them how to do it.
And it's working; this is the key.

Reclaiming the Land

Blood Diamond is a very good movie. I encourage people to see it. There
are some Hollywood aspects to it, but it is the real story of a child soldier
in a war-torn situation. The central theme of *Blood Diamonds* is, obviously, diamonds. In Sierra Leone there are large plots of land that have
been dug up for diamond mining. There are large holes everywhere in
these areas, just vast expanses of land with holes. Now, this idea didn't
come from me; it came from former child soldiers, young people in
Sierra Leone, who suggested that we use our influence to get the government to grant them the land. They wanted to reclaim it and make it
possible to grow food there.

What was once a mined-out, useless plot of land is now a rice farm.
Former child soldiers who once relied on diamonds to live can now
grow their own food to sell and eat and be self-sustainable. The future
for Africa lies in agriculture. I truly believe that very soon the time will

come when Africa will begin to support the rest of the world in more ways that one. It will be voluntary support because until now everybody's exploited Africa for centuries and they've done it violently.

A New Way of Giving

It's going to end; it's going to change; it's going to transform when we willingly give to the world in a way that is loving and peaceful, exploiting no one. The exploitation that has happened to Africa must stop.

People like to talk about aid and to feel comfortable that their governments are doing a lot. I've met people who have said, "We've given tons of money for aid over the last thirty or fifty years and Africa is still suffering." In reality, the world takes more out of Africa in debt than it contributes in aid. For every one dollar that Africa gets in international aid, seven dollars go out to pay the interest on that aid, most of which never reaches the people. It's criminal for us to continue to give international aid and rid ourselves of guilt feelings when we're actually getting more back than we're giving.

The Business of War

People talk about the wars in Africa, saying that Africans are killing Africans. We ask the question, "Where did the guns come from?" People are making big money from guns and distributing them into African countries. People got mad whenever there was a peace process underway in Liberia. Why? The contractors in Liberia who were making a lot of money from the big aid agencies knew that their jobs would come to an end. The peacekeepers that were making lots of money knew their jobs would be ending. The people who benefit from the lack of government restrictions on diamond exploitation were unhappy because their money would go away. There were so many people who did not want the wars to end.

This situation will change when you and I say: "No more. This must stop." Governments respond to people; they respond to masses. I'm going to paraphrase here, but I believe it was Eisenhower who said to someone who came to him with a policy that he absolutely loved, "I like your policy; I like your idea, but go out into the streets and fight to make me believe in what you're proposing."

If we ever want to see the end of poverty, suffering, and exploitation, we can't sit back and say, "Yes, we know it's bad." We can't just sit back and applaud when I say something that makes sense. We have to be in the streets: protesting, marching, and talking until change comes.

Justice for All

Justice will not be achieved in America until it's achieved around the world. This goes for the people in Africa, in Israel and Palestine, everywhere that people are being exploited, marginalized, and killed. Justice must come to them. And I will paraphrase Martin Luther King who said that we will never be truly at peace until all of God's children are at peace as well. That is so true.

I want to leave with a challenge to you tonight: Each and every person in this room can do so much more. If you're doing something already, that's great. But we have to challenge ourselves to do more. We have to reach out to people who don't know. Someone asked me, "Who is the greater threat — the rebel leaders who cause all these atrocities or those who sleep and don't take action?"

Power in Numbers

There was a United States ambassador to Liberia during the Liberian elections that said that there are more good people than bad people in Liberia; I truly believe that it's time for the good people to win. If you think about it, some of the worst atrocities in the world have been masterminded by just a handful of people. In Liberia you could probably count about five or ten people who were instrumental in the wars. It's the same for Rwanda, the same for most of the worst atrocities in the world.

On the flip side, there are millions who could take positive action who are doing nothing or are simply unaware. I think that's the bigger threat. If those millions of people awakened their brilliance to help change the world, we could kick out the bad guys in no time. Your challenge tonight is to find something you can do to change the world. I know we're going to have a question-and-answer session and I'll bet that someone will ask, "What can I do?" so I'm going to jump ahead of the game.

What Can I Do?

I cannot tell you what to do. The key is for every individual to find the strength, the passion, for the thing that they can do to change the world. Let no one tell you what to do. You find it; you identify it; you go out and do it. That's the most sustainable way to change the world. I found this quote from John F. Kennedy after someone told me: "Africa is too far away. Why should we be helping them?" Kennedy said in his Inaugural Address: "To those peoples in the huts and villages across the globe struggling to break the bonds of mass misery, we pledge our best efforts to help them help themselves for whatever period is required; not because the Communists may be doing it, not because we seek their votes, but because it is right. If a free society cannot help the many who are poor, it cannot save the few who are rich. We must remember that."

Thank you.

January 15, 2009
SGI-USA New York Culture of Peace Resource Center

NOTES:

1. The First Liberian Civil War was an internal conflict in Liberia from 1989 until 1997. The conflict killed more than two hundred thousand people and eventually led to the involvement of the Economic Community of West African States (ECOWAS) and of the United Nations. The peace did not last long, and in 1999 the Second Liberian Civil War broke out.

2. Charles Taylor and the National Patriotic Front of Liberia fought to overthrow the government of Samuel K. Doe. Taylor was the president of Liberia from 1997 to 2003. He has been tried for war crimes against humanity.

Pursuing Peace

The Role of Individuals in Resolving International Conflict

Anna Spain

Associate Professor of Law, University of Colorado Law School

Anna Spain is a professor, scholar, mediator, and lawyer dedicated to the cause of promoting peace. As an associate professor at the University of Colorado Law School, she teaches courses in international law, international dispute resolution, international human rights, international humanitarian law, and mediation. She researches and writes about the promotion of peace through international law. Her article, "The U.N. Security Council's Duty to Decide," published in the *Harvard National Security Journal* in 2013, received the 2014 American Society of International Law's Francis Lieber Prize (article category).

Anna has been a professional mediator since 1995 and has worked to help governments, communities, companies, universities, and families address individual and systemic conflict. Today, she remains active in various outreach organizations and engages in pro bono work close to home and around the world. Anna earned her JD from Harvard Law School and formerly served as an attorney-adviser at the U.S. Department of State where she worked on matters at the United Nations Compensation Commission and the Iran-U.S. Claims Tribunal. She is a member of the Council on Foreign Relations (Term Member), the American Society of International Law, and Mediators Beyond Borders International. Anna lives in Boulder, Colorado, with her husband and two daughters.

Anna Spain addresses several of the eight action areas defined in the 1999 United Nations Declaration and Programme of Action on a Culture of Peace, particularly the eighth, promoting international peace and security.

She spoke about how we as ordinary citizens respond to reports of conflict and actions that we can take to promote world peace. Ms. Spain states: "The thing about us as human beings is that we really are capable of changing, but each

one of us must do it ourselves. We have to be the change.
We have to be the ones who say, 'Today, I am going to do it
differently.' When you do that, you inspire those around
you to do the same thing. No one can tell you what change is
needed or how you can get involved to help create peace in
the world. You know your skills. You know your passions.
You know your capacity. What you need to know is that you
can do it and now is the time. What are you waiting for?"

(Below is the transcript of remarks made by Professor Spain at the SGI-
USA Culture of Peace Distinguished Speaker Series in Los Angeles in
2009 when she was the deputy director of the University of California,
Los Angeles Burkle Center for International Relations and a lecturer in
law at the UCLA School of Law.)

I am pleased to talk today not only about some of the grand aspects of
fostering peace between nations, but also, at a personal level, what
you can do as individuals to foster peace where you live and work.
The foundational concept unifying my talk today is this — we are all
connected. Before turning to this theme, let me first take a moment to
share with you a bit about my background and why the promotion of
peace — individually and internationally — is such a passion for me and
has been for most of my adult life.

I came to the field of conflict resolution very young. In high school I
was selected to train as a peer mediator and gained my initial experience
mediating between students who were, five minutes earlier, fighting on
the playground outside about who stole who's boyfriend and related
matters. I would invite my peers to sit down, establish ground rules,
and encourage storytelling about what happened and why. More often
than not, these teens would leave the room with a clearer understanding
about what happened and why their violent reaction was not something

they wanted to continue in the future. In the particular case of boyfriend stealing, the two girls determined that "he" was not worth it. Mediating seemed like a fairly easy line of work and I enjoyed it. Quickly, however, what seemed amusing turned quite serious.

The community where I grew up near Columbus, Ohio, had a high degree of conflict, particularly racial conflict. There were historical, deeply entrenched conflicts between the white majority and the black minority in the town, and a whole host of others trying to find a place to fit in in-between. The mayor at the time recognized that the community could not go on this way and that something needed to be done. The peer mediators who were experienced at mediating high school disputes were suddenly asked to become community mediators and facilitators to structure civil and constructive dialogue between parents, adults, colleagues, and professionals, all of whom had become a part of this very intense, and at times violent, racial conflict.

We (the high school mediators) were, if you will, forged in the fire, but through that formative experience, from such an early age, I saw the power of people to change. People have the power to make new choices to ensure that their future is different from their past. This change can be achieved through many means, but I want to talk about just one of those means, the power of conflict resolution (through methods such as mediation, facilitation, and negotiation) to promote positive peaceful change among people and between nations.

When we turn on CNN, we might see Anderson Cooper describing what is going on in our world. When we are faced with viewing international crises, war, conflict, challenges, or economic recession, we have a choice to make as a viewer. How will we respond to such, often overwhelming, negativity? Will we retreat into safety where we can find it, or will we reach out, through empathy or perhaps by taking constructive measures to assist those who are suffering?

I had an experience the summer of 2008 when I was with my husband in Germany, visiting my parents who lived there. We turned on the television to see that armed conflict had broken out between Russia and Georgia. What I saw on the television was shocking because it was not the sort of coverage I had grown used to seeing in the United States. They showed death. They showed blood. They showed raw, unadulterated trauma. It occurred to me that in this country we are blessed with having the Atlantic on one side and the Pacific on the other. It gives us a sense of security. Looking at CNN International while I was in Germany, the conflict felt close by, not separated by distance. I realized that distance, whether physical or emotional, separates people. Distance allows us to separate from one another in the world. It allows us to create boundaries that keep people apart, based on ideals, on beliefs, or on culture and tradition. Conflict resolution is all about looking critically at these boundaries, and understanding when we need them and when they are artificial or destructive.

This brings me to the central theme of this talk today. It is not quite right to believe we are as disconnected as we may believe. We live in the era of globalization. We have great global innovations, technologies like the Internet that connect us to one another, anywhere and at any time. We also live in the era where resources and population growth demand that we think more broadly about our communities, not just as the neighborhood and street where we live, but about the impact we have on one another, even when the "one another" is far away. In America, in particular, we have to pay particular attention to how we affect the world.

One example is how we buy, use, and waste a resource; so let's pick one. Think about water. Bottled water is very popular now. My grandfather used to laugh and say, "In my day, if anyone would actually pay for a bottle of water, they would be thought of as nuts." But we do it today, because it is healthy for us and because we like to drink water. But if we think about where that water comes from and how it gets to us, that one bottle quenching our thirst takes a lot of resources to make. The production of plastic itself not only requires many resources and inputs, but also emits pollution, carbon monoxide, sulfur dioxide, and carbon dioxide. How does it get to us? It comes on a truck or by sea. This requires fossil fuel consumption. Then we drink the water and throw away the bottle, which often ends up in a landfill or in the ocean.

According to one study based on the U.S. Environmental Protection Agency's data, Americans throw away at least fifty million plastic water bottles every day.[1] Now you may be thinking, yes, I know, we are all guilty. The central question is this: Can knowledge of one's contribution to a problem motivate change? If I know that I am contributing to severe plastic water bottle waste is that enough to cause me to actually change my behavior? And you may also be thinking, what does all this have to do with international conflict anyway? I am about to tell you.

Ban Ki-moon, the secretary-general of the United Nations, has often said that, in his estimation, climate change is the greatest threat facing the future, because climate change exacerbates scarcity of the resources humans need to survive, one of which is water. One-third of the world's population doesn't have access to safe drinking water, so when you and I choose to use water in this way, we're making choices for other people about resources that they can or can't use. This is just one of the many cycles of influence we have. Living in this country brings great benefits and privileges, and we should be very proud, but it also comes with great responsibility. How can we apply this sense of responsibility to the international events we see on CNN?

What I have learned in the field of conflict resolution is that, in order to solve something, you must first take a step back and assess the root causes. For example, we can take any of the world's conflicts. We can look at Rwanda and the genocide that happened there, and we can look at more recent events; we can look at the conflict in Gaza or in the Democratic Republic of Congo. It's easy for us, being far away, having distance, to come up in our own minds with what we think is going on, but how do we assess root causes of conflict? How do you as regular citizens make up your mind about your reaction to such events?

There are some changes happening on the international stage that should bring us great hope and, moreover, great reason to hope. International law has recently put forth a new concept, coined the "Responsibility to Protect"[2] doctrine, also known as R2P. It embodies the fundamental principle I am discussing here today, that we are all connected. R2P redefines the concept of sovereignty by stating that individual nations are entitled to the rights afforded by sovereignty (e.g. the right of a nation to be free from external interference into its internal affairs) but are also held to uphold a responsibility to protect its own people from certain international crimes and mass atrocities. When a nation is unwilling or unable to protect its own, its sovereignty becomes limited allowing the international community to intervene in order to provide such protection. The R2P doctrine gives legal and ethical justification for outside coalitions to intervene when a nation is not protecting its own people from certain harms.

This concept is relatively new. It was established in 2001, and was accepted by numerous nations at the World Summit in 2005 and recognized by the United Nations Security Council in 2006 and 2009, but it remains to be seen what responsibility to protect (R2P) can do to promote peace, reduce conflict, and bring about reconciliation in our world. What outside groups will intervene? Will it be one country, like the United States? Should it be a coalition of the international community? Could it be international NGOs? Who has the right to intervene, and on whose behalf? R2P is not without controversy. It should not be used to justify colonial motivations. However, it represents an emerging global consensus that we are all connected, and we cannot turn a blind eye to certain grave tragedies that are happening in a far away land to people who are strangers to ourselves.

This dialogue is happening at a very high level among states, but it has ramifications for us. Right now at this very moment we can look at the world map and see places that are affected by armed conflict resulting in humanitarian crises and mass atrocities. In 2014, we can look to the people suffering as a result of the civil war in Syria where a chemical gas known as sarin has allegedly been used or the people in Syria, Iraq, and Turkey facing an expanding Islamic State, which gives them the "convert or die" option. The consequences of ongoing conflict in South Sudan, the Democratic Republic of Congo, and the Central African Republic threaten the lives of millions. Intervention into these countries has been inconsistent. We must consider who has the responsibility to protect those who can't protect themselves? Do we? If we do, as individuals, what can we do? We're not states, we don't have negotiating power at the international body authorized to make such a decision like the United Nations Security Council? What is our responsibility?

We know some of the ways because we have faced them time and time again. You can donate. Americans are blessed to have more resources than most people. You can become an activist and get involved. You can use the skills you have, whether you are an interviewer, whether you can write, whether you have great Internet research capabilities, whether you are a very good at advocating and raising awareness. You can find your passion and use your skills to get involved in some way. We are all busy. Maybe sometimes you have an hour, maybe sometimes you have a day. If we all do what we can where we can, then we can start to see change.

I want to talk about a third way — between that of an individual and that of the international community — that is not often discussed. This third way to effect change and promote peace is something I refer to as the individual operating within the international system. When I had the opportunity to serve as a U.S. delegate to the United Nations, it was in the Geneva U.N. building. It has a special place called the Serpentine Bar. The Serpentine Bar is this gorgeous 1960s-era coffee shop, if you will, that is in the shape of an *s*. When you walk in you see people from every possible corner of the planet, looking every possible different way — different outfits, different colors, different shapes, different sizes. They are all diplomats representing their nations with pride and engaging in constructive and problem-solving dialogue with one another. There are literally, on any given day at the United Nations, more than a hundred different forums working together trying to solve problems across borders, so it is very international, it is state to state, but there is also something important about each individual there. We have seen that, when organizations and countries have good leaders, great things can happen, but when these individuals are not in a good position to lead, bad things can happen. Thus, the individual does matter, even at the state level. It was something I didn't realize until I saw it with my own eyes — the power of the individual.

What is it about individuals that can make a difference? I was blessed to be told this story by a colleague of mine who is a mediator. He was asked to go to West Africa to help settle a long-standing tribal dispute. One group of people had been the dominant force in the region; they controlled most of the land and most of the resources. The underdog was a younger group with poor leadership who kept using guerilla tactics to take resources away from the dominant group. The mediator was an American. He came in and met with the parties in advance and then he arranged for them both to show up at one location for the mediation.

He brought them into the room and all of a sudden the chief of the dominant tribe stood up. He was very angry and he stomped his foot and said to them: "How dare you, how dare YOU, mediator, bring me here to talk with these people and they don't even have someone at my level worthy of hearing me. How dare you!" The mediator sat back and thought, *uh oh, I must have blown it. What should I do now?* The room was silent. One minute, two minutes went by, but this is the beauty of mediation. Sometimes it doesn't matter who the mediator is, because the process of bringing people together with the aim of solving problems has unique and unexpected ways of working. Here, the leader of the other tribe, a twenty-something young man, walked over to the chief, kneeled down. He said: "Oh great Chief, you are so right. It is precisely because we have no one at your status, because we have no great chief, no leader, that we have this problem. You see, we lost all of our leaders to the great war. We have no one to guide us and to provide wisdom. This is why we are disorganized. This is why we are stealing your resources. Great Chief, please help us!" The chief looked down, put his hand under the young man's chin and raised his face and looked in his eyes and said: "No, it is you who are the great one, for you have helped me realize the power of forgiveness. I ask you to forgive me." That was the mediation. The mediator had very little to do with it.

This was such a powerful story when I heard it, because it is an example of how each one of us has our own way to promote peace. How do we do this? First, we must remember that we are indeed connected, but second, we must remember that there is something about the energy of a person committed to peace that can make a greater difference. We have many examples. I will raise a few.

There is a former UCLA student who has now graduated. His name is Adam Sterling. When he was at UCLA,[3] he took up the cause of Darfur. He couldn't understand why governments weren't moving more quickly. He couldn't understand why people would care, but not take action. He dedicated himself to doing something. I think we can all relate because we have those moments where we read the news or we see something happening, and think, *gosh, I should do something, but what*? He did something; he singlehandedly started a movement, The Sudan Divestment Task Force. After a few years of severe hard work and pounding the pavement, he got the likes of George Clooney and Don Cheadle to support him and he marched that campaign all the way to Capitol Hill.[4] That's how, as one person, he was able to make a real difference.

Here's another example — Uganda. The Lord's Resistance Army in Uganda over the years has taken at least three hundred thousand children as child soldiers.[5] Unfortunately, this is a common practice to ensure a source of fighters. These kids, six years old to fifteen or sixteen years on up are turned mentally, psychologically, emotionally, and physically into fighters. So what can someone sitting in my home state of Ohio do to help these kids? Well, someone figured out a way. Three American college students (Jason Russell, Bobby Bailey, and Laren Poole) started the Invisible Children Bracelet Campaign and organized the communities in Uganda to create these bracelets.[6] They made them out of the resources they had and shipped them to the United States and started to sell them. The money has gone directly to each former child soldier and helped them to re-integrate by getting them training, school, education, and counseling so that they can become productive members of their former community. It took one person, or in this case three, who said, "Hey, what can I do?" They had an idea and did it.

This spirit of realistic optimism drives the human impulse to pursue change and to turn empathy into constructive action. I encountered such spirit in 2008, when I was lucky enough to get a ticket to the 2008 presidential inauguration. I flew in the day before. It was eleven degrees at seven in the morning with the wind chill. It was freezing. We were all packed in there like sardines, marching down to the Capitol. But you know what? I saw people there in their nineties. I saw six-year-olds. I saw every color, every background. I saw Americans, and I saw people from around the world. People were freezing their butts off, but they were happy to be there, really happy to be there. I met people who didn't make it down in time and who got stuck on the Metro, people who were lost, and people who weren't able to break through some crowded access point. Instead of being bitter, they were just happy to be a part of something larger than themselves — which many of them described as a commitment to and hope for a better future.

The thing about us as human beings is that we really are capable of changing, but each one of us must do it ourselves. We have to be the change. We have to be the ones who say, "Today, I am going to do it differently." When you do that, you inspire those around you to do the same thing. No one can tell you what change is needed or how you can get involved to help create peace in the world. You know your skills. You know your passions. You know your capacity. What you need to know is that you can do it and now is the time. What are we waiting for?

My last example of a great leader and someone who affected change as an individual is somebody we're all familiar with and that is Mahatma Gandhi. He advised this: "If we could change ourselves, the tendencies in the world would also change. As a man changes his own nature, so does the attitude of the world change toward him.... We need not wait to see what others do."[7] This message is simple but also difficult to do. Why was Gandhi so successful at it? He lived during a time of great change and conflict when India was emerging from colonialism after decades of brutal violence. During World War II, the entire world thought things would never be the same. Somehow this one person was able to find something within himself to rise to the challenge and be a source of positivity and hope. Everyone around him was skeptical, and saying: "Are you crazy, look at what's happening? You want us to believe in peace?" But he believed, and because he believed, more people believed, and because they believed, still more came on board. Decades later, it is easy for us to look back historically and say, "Ah, yes, he was one of the greats." We have had other great examples as well, but to be that one person in that moment of deep skepticism when scary things are happening, to find that thing inside of you and say "I can do this" is something we can all achieve when we adopt a different attitude.

It is interesting that this Culture of Peace lecture is happening this year (2009). In 1999, the United Nations came up with the Declaration on a Culture of Peace, and announced that this would be a decade of great peace. Looking back at almost the decade's end, the first decade of the new century, we have seen that this has been a challenging decade for many reasons. It has been a decade where a lot of us have fallen into our fears. There are scary things that are happening in the world. There is conflict. There is war. We faced a recession, and it affected many of us. Terrorism has changed many aspects of everyday lives including security at airports. There is nothing that each one of us can singularly do to change all of that, but what we can do is decide what type of person we are going to be in the face of challenge. Are we going to be the type of person that allows fear to get the best of us, shut down, protect what we have, or are we going to be the type of person to reach out, inspire, and find a way to solve these problems and address these challenges?

That is what my work has been about as a mediator, and as somebody who teaches conflict resolution to others. In the face of skepticism, you have to search for ways to believe that the future can be better. Hopelessness will get us nowhere; it does not solve problems. Skepticism can be useful, because it helps us critically assess where we went wrong, but don't let it prevent us from finding the solutions we all seek. If as individuals we can delve deep into ourselves to find this inner source, this inner ability to change and inspire, that can be powerful. There is something called the "collective consciousness." It is a term created in the late 1800s by French social theorist Émile Durkheim to convey the idea that beliefs and ideas can spread across a society and influence behavior. Some of you may have read Malcolm Gladwell's book, *The Tipping Point*. He comes up with three ideas about collective consciousness. He says that ideas can spread just like a virus: because of contagiousness, because little causes can have big effects, and because change happens, sometimes not gradually, but because a buildup gets us to that point where things "tip," or spread rapidly.

On Election Day, I was on the UCLA campus teaching a class. It was about eleven in the morning. Everyone all of a sudden starting saying: "Obama won! He must have won. He has won!" It was spreading rapidly to all the students, all the staff, to the entire campus. I started to think about it. Some of these people really wanted Hillary Clinton. Some were huge John McCain supporters. It wasn't politics. There was a palpable sense that something else had happened. The polls had not yet closed on the East Coast. Nobody knew for sure that he had won, but everybody started to sense something.

What if, just like the Internet, humans are already connected through our collective consciousness? What if it's more than a theory? What if it's a way we can really influence one another's behavior? Then, does your responsibility to find inner peace, to promote it where you live, with the people you know, not become incredibly important and powerful? What if there really is a tipping point, when enough people do one simple thing and things tip? This is not to abdicate the responsibility at the state level. Nations still need to do a good job to prevent conflict and to manage, mitigate, and to resolve it. But we individuals have a role to play too. We can't simply wait for our leaders and the international community to do something. We can do something too. We can do it today. We can do it tomorrow. We can inspire one person. We can inspire ten. In that way, one small act seemingly becomes very powerful and very contagious because we are connected. As this next century evolves, we are going to start to see that through our global economy, through our global environment, and through all the things that do connect us.

My mission as a professor, as a mediator, and as a simple citizen who really cares about this stuff, is to make sure that we are paying attention and we are awake so that we don't have to wait for our economy or for our climate to tell us that we're connected. We can understand that now, and we can start to be, as Gandhi advised, the change we seek to see in the world.

In closing, I wish to quote from one of our greats, Robert F. Kennedy.

> Each time a man stands up for an ideal, or acts to improve the lot of others, or strikes out against injustice, he sends forth a tiny ripple of hope, and crossing each other from a million different centers of energy and daring those ripples build a current which can sweep down the mightiest walls of oppression and resistance.[8]

So, I say to you my fellow citizens, be a ripple of hope and be it today.

January 31, 2009
SGI-USA Santa Monica Culture of Peace Resource Center

NOTES:

1. Pristine Planet Study available at http://www.pristineplanet.com/eco-info/How-many-plastic-water-bottles-are-thrown-away-every-day.asp (last visited November 1, 2014).

2. U.N. Office of the Special Adviser on the Prevention of Genocide available at http://www.un.org/en/preventgenocide/adviser/responsibility.shtml (last visited on November 1, 2014). R2P is an emerging norm in international law that aims to address the international community's failure to prevent and stop genocide and mass atrocities.

3. Sterling joined the fledgling Darfur Action Committee, which helped raise awareness by writing letters to the president and Congress, bringing speakers to campus and, yes, passing out fliers on Bruin Walk. The result was a proposal for the University of California to implement a policy of divestment. To generate support,

the student activists traveled to other UC campuses and bused 200 students to a Regents' meeting at UC San Diego. In March 2006, the Board of Regents adopted a model of "targeted divestment" that focuses on the worst-offending companies doing business in Sudan, making the University of California the first public educational institution to take such action. Six months later, Governor Arnold Schwarzenegger, flanked by Sterling and actor-activists Don Cheadle and George Clooney, signed two divestment-related bills into California law. http://alumni.ucla.edu/share/alumni-stories/stories/adam-sterling.aspx.

4. http://magazine.ucla.edu/depts/quicktakes/out_of_africa_darfur_genocide/.
5. http://invisiblechildren.com/our-story/.
6. http://www.youtube.com/watch?v=KvhooJ9c1Rw.
7. Mahatma Gandhi, *The Collected Works of M. K. Gandhi* (The Publications Division, New Delhi, India, 1924) (reprinted by Obscure Press, 2006).
8. Robert F. Kennedy, Public Address, *Day of Affirmation*, University of Cape Town, Cape Town, South Africa (June 6, 1966) available at http://www.rfksafilm.org/html/speeches/unicape.php (last visited November 1, 2014).

The Purposes of International Justice

David Kaye

Clinical Professor of Law,
University of California, Irvine School of Law

David Kaye is the executive director of the University of California, Los Angeles School of Law International Human Rights Program. He teaches international human rights and directs an international human rights clinic. For more than a decade, Mr. Kaye served as an international lawyer with the U.S. State Department, responsible for issues as varied as human rights, international humanitarian law, the use of force international organizations, international litigation and claims, nuclear nonproliferation, sanctions law and policy, and U.S. foreign relations law. He was a legal adviser to the American Embassy in The Hague, where he worked with the international criminal tribunals and acted as counsel to the United States in several cases before the International Court of Justice and the Iran-U.S. Claims Tribunal. From 1999 to 2002, he was the principal staff attorney on humanitarian law, handling issues such as the application of the law to detainees in Guantanamo Bay and serving on several U.S. delegations to international negotiations and conferences. The State Department honored him with four of its prestigious Superior Honor Awards.

Mr. Kaye has taught courses in international law and human rights at Georgetown University and Whittier Law School. He has also written numerous articles and book chapters in the area of international human rights.

David Kaye speaks compellingly about many of the eight action areas defined in the 1999 United Nations Declaration and Programme of Action on a Culture of Peace, but namely, the third, promoting respect for all human rights, and the eighth, promoting international peace and security.

Speaking on the topic of international justice, Mr. Kaye discusses the rule of international law as a tool to deal with the violence and injustices around the world.

Mr. Kaye states: "The rule of law is a tool that has been increasingly developed, particularly since the end of the Cold War, even though it began at the International Military

Tribunal at Nuremberg in 1945 and 1946. But, at the root, it is about holding individuals accountable for crimes, whether they pull the trigger and kill one, two, ten, or twenty people in a particular massacre, or whether they are way at the top of the political pyramid and order the death of tens of thousands of individuals."

I want to do an overview of international justice today, and also press us a bit and make us ask and answer questions as to what is international justice, why do we have it, and what good does it do?

Let me start by introducing or setting the scene. The world today obviously remains a place of deep conflict from Afghanistan to Zimbabwe, from Burma to Columbia, from Iraq to the Congo. There is war and violence, and with this war and with this violence, there are not only criminal activities by individuals, soldiers, citizens, and civilians who commit acts of violence, but there is also systematic policy-driven violence against civilians and against combatants.

The international community, and that is a phrase often used without a lot of meaning, but the international community comprises governments, international organizations, nongovernmental organizations, such as Human Rights Watch, Human Rights First, SGI, individual activists, and everybody who makes up the international community. Together we have a variety of tools at our disposal in order to deal with this kind of violence; from the shaming of individuals who are committing crimes to economic sanctions all the way to military intervention, which under international law may be authorized by the United Nations Security Council.

There is another tool we have, and it is this other tool that I want to talk about today, and that is the rule of law. The rule of law is a tool that has been increasingly developed, particularly since the end of the Cold War, even though it has its roots in the Nuremberg trials at the

International Military Tribunal in 1945 and 1946. But at the root, it is about holding individuals accountable for crimes, whether they pull the trigger and kill one, two, ten, or twenty people in a particular massacre, or, at the top of the political pyramid, order the deaths of tens of thousands of individuals.

I am going to talk about that process — the process of bringing law to a situation where we think law doesn't normally operate. Cicero said essentially that, in times of war, the law is silent, but in the face of arms, there is no law. We know that is not true. Whether it works, and whether it is effective in ending crimes and ending violence, is another question and we will be talking about that, but I am going to talk about the introduction of law in time of war.

First, I will introduce some of the institutions of international justice. I will then try to pick apart contemporary international justice and ask the questions: Why do we have it? Why do we have international justice? Why do we have institutions? What are the purposes? Does it do good? Does it do good always, sometimes, never? What is the point and why do we have it? At the end, I will invite some questions so we can then move forward in our understanding of international justice.

I will start with a specific time — July 2008. Two different events happened within the space of a week that really brought the issue of international justice to the fore. It was mid- to late July, before the Democratic or Republican conventions, when the news cycles were slow, but newspapers were dominated by stories of international justice. I will talk about two of them.

The first is Darfur. It's July 17 in Khartoum, the capital of Sudan. As I suspect everyone knows about the conflict in the Western part of Darfur, the Western part of Sudan. Much of the severe violence has been in the news over many years.

This time, however, it wasn't about the violence per se. It was in the news because a prosecutor in The Hague, the seat of government in the Netherlands, had decided to seek an arrest warrant against the president of Sudan, Omar al-Bashir.

The prosecutor's name is Luis Moreno Ocampo; he is the chief prosecutor of the International Criminal Court (ICC), which I will talk about later. He alleged that al-Bashir bore responsibility for crimes against humanity, war crimes, and, the heart of his claim, genocide against civilians in Darfur.

He sought an arrest warrant. He didn't just seek an arrest warrant for some individual who might have been a member of the Janjaweed Militia, the militia that has done much of the killing in Darfur, although he has also sought arrest warrants for Janjaweed leaders. He didn't seek an arrest warrant just for somebody who had raped women or killed individuals in the camps or the villages of Darfur, he went straight to the top. He said that Omar al-Bashir, as president of Sudan, bears the ultimate responsibility for what is going on in Darfur. He said he bears the ultimate responsibility for the genocide, as he defines it, crimes against humanity, and war crimes. He asked the court to issue an arrest warrant against Bashir, a sitting head of state; Bashir is still the president of Sudan.

In March 2009, as you might recall, a three-judge panel of the ICC accepted Ocampo's arguments, and actually issued an arrest warrant. There is now an arrest warrant that has been issued for Omar al-Bashir, and I don't want to get into the legalities quite yet as to whether that's likely to be implemented, but since March, he has been under the threat of arrest. Within a week of the al-Bashir arrest warrant request, a remarkable thing occurred. Serbian police in Belgrade, the capital of Serbia, arrested a homeopathic healer practicing in Belgrade. The healer went by the name of Dragan Dabic, but he had another name too; he had a real name, which is Radovan Karadzic. When I teach human rights, or international justice at UCLA, most of my students were of elementary school age at the time of the war in Bosnia, but for any of us who lived during that time, the name Radovan Karadzic is one of these striking names of individuals who were responsible for most of the carnage in Bosnia between 1991 and 1995.

Karadzic had been indicted in 1994 by the International Criminal Tribunal in the former Yugoslavia, the ICTY, which we will also talk about later. He had been sought by the North Atlantic Treaty Organization (NATO) for several years. It was thought that Karadzic had been on the run in the mountains, and in the monasteries of Montenegro or Serbia, maybe even in the Serbian part of Bosnia, but low and behold he was right under the noses of security forces in Serbia. My guess is that they knew that he was there for many years because as soon as there was a change of government to a liberal government in Serbia, within a month, Karadzic was arrested and sent to The Hague for trial.

Soon he will stand trial for crimes against humanity, war crimes, and genocide that occurred in Bosnia between 1991 and 1995, including the massacre at Srebrenica in July of 1995, which killed somewhere around eight thousand Bosnian Muslim boys and men. He will also be tried for his responsibility for Secret Sarajevo, which also left thousands of people dead between 1991 and 1995.[1]

So as a result, during this preconvention media lull in July 2008, U.S. and international newspapers were dominated by this question of international justice. Why is it that we were going after these senior leaders? Why were we going after Radon Karadzic years after the war ended? Why are we going after al-Bashir in the midst of conflict? How do we go after these people? What is the purpose of international justice? What's it all about?

I will talk about what it is all about, first, by describing the scene and then asking some questions about it. What are the crimes at issue? International criminal justice is mainly about justice for the victims. It is also about other things — security, accountability, but at its root, it is about accountability for three kinds of crimes. It's about accountability for crimes against humanity, which is described as essentially systematic and widespread attacks and maltreatment of civilian populations. They can also be combatants and victims as well — crimes against humanity.

These are pictures of individuals — and pictures were taken and some of you may have read about the trials of a torturer, really the lead torturer of the Khmer Rouge, a man who goes by the name of Duch. Before each of the torture sessions at which these individuals were killed, pictures were taken of them and these pictures (referring to photographs in a PowerPoint presentation) are collected in the museum in Phnom Penh. That first picture in the upper left hand corner is a snapshot. These crimes against humanity were massive, systematic crimes against civilians.

Another category is war crimes, crimes that take place against civilians, against combatants, and against interned people whether they are civilians or combatants. They are violations of the Geneva Convention of 1949, such as torture, maltreatment of prisoners of war, murder of protected persons such as civilians or detainees. Those are war crimes. These tribunals that we're talking about have jurisdiction over war crimes in addition to crimes against humanity.

Finally, there is genocide. Genocide is defined as a number of acts — killing, serious harm, all intended to destroy in whole or in part, national ethnic or religious groups. Genocide, more than just about any other crime in the international community, is about a crime of policy. It's about a kind of crime that is directed against an entire population with the intent of wiping it out.

There are many legal issues about whether genocide is too narrowly defined under jurisprudence today, and I don't want to get into that necessarily. Suffice it to say that genocide in international law is an extremely difficult thing to prove. It's much easier to prove crimes against humanity or war crimes because you don't have to go into the mind of the person who committed the crime and ask: Did they intend to destroy in whole or in part this particular group?

These kinds of crimes are not new to the international community. War crimes, and crimes against humanity in particular, are not new. Genocide wasn't defined until 1948. Nuremberg changed things. In the wake of the Holocaust, in the wake of the massive crimes of the Nazis during World War II, publics in the West, and in particular, publics among the Allies, sensed that inaction against Nazi leaders simply was not going to be an option. In past conflicts, those who committed crimes were either executed on the spot, which is actually what Winston Churchill wanted to do around 1943 or 1944. He felt that the Allies should just execute the senior Nazi leaders. That's the way it had been done. Either people went to their death in front of a firing squad or they went to a villa in the South of France.

Franklin Delano Roosevelt, in particular, and a number of other senior leaders, thought that wasn't going to be the appropriate way to deal with Nazi leaders; there needed to be a different mechanism. They had to do something that actually would allow this moment at the end of World War II to be used as a teaching moment. The Allies in 1945 opted for the International Military Tribunal at Nuremberg.

They created a charter in which they decided that they were not just going to execute these Nazi leaders. They might come to that by the end of the process, but they were going to get there by law. They wanted to state that the Nazis deciding that law didn't matter, or that the law being what the Nazis decided the law would be, was a deeply illegitimate kind of law. In a weird way the Nazis were extremely bureaucratic and based their actions on a kind of law, but the Tribunal was going to say that that kind of lawmaking is inappropriate. The international community still to this day wants the rule of law to make accountable those who commit crimes against humanity, war crimes, and crimes of genocide.

Justice Robert Jackson served as the leading justice at Nuremberg. Now, we see these trials as a triumph of law over vengeance, but at the time, and even today, there is discussion by people who wonder if this was really just a show trial, or if it was a kind of victor's justice.

In fact, at the end of Nuremberg, essentially a little more than a year-long trial against twenty-six senior Nazis, three were acquitted, twelve were sentenced to death, and several others were sentenced to terms of ten years to life in prison. Nuremberg was then followed by a series of trials in the military sectors of Germany following the war, including U.S. Military Tribunals that tried a number of Nazi leaders. Then they were followed even after that by trials in domestic courts around Europe. In April 2009, we saw the continuing relevance of the Nazi era in the deportation of John Demjanjuk, who is accused of running the Sobibor camp, and sending him back to Germany, but no tribunal. No system of international justice followed for essentially fifty years. It was Nuremberg, and Nuremberg was over in 1946. Individual countries did their own thing for a number of years, but until 1993, there was essentially nothing that went on in the world of international justice.

There was a lot of thinking about how we prepare for the time when we might have courts that would bring accountability for these kinds of crimes, but essentially there is a moment that is frozen in terms of international law, and that's 1946 with the trials in Nuremberg. The legacy of Nuremberg has been more or less dormant for fifty years.

Today is much different. I want you to fast forward from 1946 in Germany all the way to Bosnia in 1992. Anybody who looks at the international response to the war in Bosnia can only conclude that the international community was essentially hamstrung and didn't know what to do. It didn't want to intervene militarily for fear of losing its own soldiers. We are essentially talking about NATO, European states, and the

United States. They didn't want to intervene, and it was clear in the context of the end of the Cold War that they weren't going to be able to get authorization, that is, the West wasn't going to be able to get authorization in the U.N. Security Council from the Russians in order to intervene in Bosnia against the Serbs or in Croatia against the Serbs.

There was essentially inaction in the international community. There were little band-aids here and there. There were safe havens created in cities and towns throughout Bosnia, but if you go all the way to 1995 to Srebrenica, we saw that these safe havens were anything but safe. They were simply overrun by the Serbs in time.

In 1992 and 1993 a thought started, that if we're not going to do anything in terms of military intervention to actually stop the war, let's at least assert our abhorrence of the tactics being used by the Serbs and on both sides. If you look at the numbers, it was more by the Serbs. At the same time the United Nations imposed an arms embargo — so we were not really even allowing the Bosniaks, the Bosnian Muslims to fight back in the war. This started a process in 1992 and 1993 to create an international tribunal that was modeled more or less on Nuremberg. In 1992 Europe saw the worst crimes on its territory since World War II, and they decided to actually create something that uses that legacy of Nuremberg and create international justice for themselves.

In 1993, during the Bosnian War, the United Nations decided to create an international tribunal. It's going to be able to punish war crimes, crimes against humanity, and genocide.

In 1994, and beginning for a period of one hundred days, violence happened that the world really hadn't seen on a scale since Pol Pot in Cambodia, and that was the genocide in Rwanda. Within one hundred days, somewhere between five hundred thousand or six hundred thousand and eight hundred thousand Rwandans were massacred in the most brutal ways. The United Nations, which had just created the ICTY, the Yugoslavian Tribunal, decided to create the International Criminal Tribunal for Rwanda (ICTR), a tribunal for Rwanda.

These are tribunals that were created ad hoc. They were created to deal with very specific situations, specific crimes, specific conflicts, and a specific moment in time. In 1993 there was the ICTY, and in 1994, the ICTR in Rwanda. The international community started to see that these were needed since these massive conflicts emerged all around the world, but at the same time, every time these institutions are created, it is expensive. Institutions were created in The Hague, with the Yugoslavian tribunal, and down in Arusha, Tanzania, for the Rwanda tribunal.

As of 2009 the ICTY had logged 1.5 billion dollars, give or take a few hundred million. The Rwanda tribunal wasn't very far behind. These were very expensive operations. The international community, the activists, but also some governments, started to push forward for permanent international status. Why do these ad hoc? Why not make them permanent so that, whenever there is conflict, we can have a standing court that can deal with these kinds of crimes; that is how the International Criminal Court came into being by a statute approved by more than a hundred countries in Rome in 1998, and famously, the United States wasn't among them.

We can talk about the reasons for that, but the ICC now exists. It has existed since 2002, when sixty states agreed to it, and it entered into force. Now it has 108 states. Sean Butler here today is the head of the International Criminal Court Alliance Coalition in Los Angeles. It is a party to the International Criminal Court, and it is a real institution. It is pursuing cases against the Lord's Resistance Army, the brutal organization that operates in Northern Uganda; and it is pursuing cases in Darfur as mentioned, in the Democratic Republic of the Congo, one of these quieter genocides — not so quiet for the people who live in the Congo, where millions of people have been killed, up to perhaps five million — and, the Central African Republic is pursuing a case as well.

Since that time, since the mid-1990s, we have had other tribunals. We have had a tribunal that was established for Sierra Leone. A special court was also developed for Cambodia dealing with the crimes of the Khmer Rouge. These are not ad hoc tribunals created by the United Nations, but these are tribunals created by agreement between these states and the United Nations to create what we call hybrid tribunals, that are a bit international, in that they have international civil servants who are involved in helping to prosecute cases, but they are creatures of domestic law as well. They are part of the domestic criminal justice system, and there are other courts as well.

I also included domestic courts; there is a picture (referring to a photograph in a PowerPoint presentation) of the U.S. Supreme Court, because, even though I am talking about international tribunals, obviously these are the kinds of crimes that can be tried from the domestic courts in the places where they occurred. There is a large school of thought, a very vibrant school of thought, that this is where all of these crimes should be tried. They should be tried by the victims in the places where these crimes actually occurred. Bring the justice closer to the people who suffered. Domestic courts around the world can try cases as well. The U.S. courts under something called the Alien Court Statute can actually place civil liability on torturers and others who are responsible for crimes against humanity and war crimes and such. It's important to keep in mind that although we are talking about international tribunals, these kinds of cases can be tried in domestic courts as well.

Who are the defendants? This has been a big problem for the ICTY and the ICTR. It's clearly an emerging problem for the ICC as well. Do you try what they called in the Yugoslavian tribunal, "the low hanging fruit," the trigger pullers, those who aren't protected by a political party or organized crime, the way some of these big time political leaders are. They are easier to capture. It's a lot easier to capture a guy like Dusko Tadic, who was the first person arrested and sent to The Hague for trial by the ICTY, the Yugoslavian tribunal, because he was traveling in Germany and some Bosnian Muslim recognized him as someone who was at a camp where this guy stayed. He is arrested in Germany and sent to The Hague. That's not going to happen to Slobodan Milosevic. It's not going to happen to Radovan Karadzic. There are other ways of getting to those people, but it takes a lot of time and effort, and a lot of energy.

Over time, it has become clear to the international community that these courts cannot be used for trying these low hanging fruit. There are just too many of them. In Bosnia, for example, let's say a conservative estimate of the number of people killed during the war is somewhere around one hundred thousand. The figures are really one hundred thousand to five hundred thousand. But even using the lower number of one hundred thousand, that's not five, ten, fifteen, or even two hundred people doing the killing, that's thousands of people committing crimes. The estimates provided indicate that there are something like three thousand or four thousand individuals who committed crimes during the war. I don't mean just like theft, I mean a war crime or someone who participated in crimes against humanity. Are you going to go after all those people? You might, but that's going to be expensive. Only 161 people have been indicted by the Yugoslavian tribunal; 161 people and it cost 1.5 billion dollars. We can't go after all of those people because it will make that 1.5 billion dollar number pale by comparison. Instead, over time, the international community has realized that you need to essentially divide up responsibility. The international community can go after the senior level people, essentially, to make an assertion of values. If you are going to be a leader of a country, you have to adhere to certain norms. If you don't, and you commit these kinds of crimes, you are going to be tried by the international community.

Here is a picture (referring to a photograph in a PowerPoint presentation) of Radovan Karadzic standing with Ratko Mladic, the last remaining big fish for the Yugoslavian tribunal. He was the general who was responsible for most of the carnage during the war in Bosnia.

Here is another picture (referring to a photograph in a PowerPoint presentation) is of Duch, the man I mentioned who was torturer in chief for the Khmer Rouge during the war in Cambodia.

The international community goes after those kinds of people. We are not going to see trials any longer at an international level of the low hanging fruit of individual soldiers. It's possible we might if those individuals commit such massive crimes that they can really only be tried by an international tribunal, but the focus on individuals more and more is being left to domestic courts. There is a division of labor; the international community takes the senior leaders, and domestic courts take the lower level leaders.

I have already mentioned a few of these different players in these tribunals. We have the victims, we have the crimes, we have the defendants, and we also have the prosecutors, of course. The prosecutors at these tribunals have come from all around the world, although, more often than not, they have come from the West.

In another picture (referring to a photograph in a PowerPoint presentation), you see Louise Arbour, the high commissioner for human rights. Just a few years ago, she was the second chief prosecutor of the ICTY. In the middle of the war in Kosovo, exactly ten years ago, she indicted Slobodan Milosevic. Indicting the president of a country in the middle of a war was a risky move. She was perceived as a maverick — that would be the word we would use today. The idea that she could prosecute or indict somebody in the middle of a war raised these questions: What if we are headed toward the peace process? What do we do then with Slobodan Milosevic? Since Milosevic is now an indicted criminal, an indicted war criminal, it will be a lot harder for others to negotiate or shake his hand in negotiation and try to figure out how to move forward. Suddenly international justice became a player and the international tribunal was a player in international politics.

Now we will launch into the question period. Instead of talking only about what the international tribunals are, I want to transition to talking about their purposes and why we have them, and whether we think they are a good thing. I am working with a documentary filmmaker named Edward Nachtrieb, who has made some wonderful films. He is interested in the issue of the impact of international justice, the impact on the ground, all this stuff we are talking about, men in robes, or generals wearing fatigues, or what not. How does trying these people actually make a difference and what is the point of it? This is less than ten minutes, a sample reel of interviews for the film we're making, and then we will talk about the purpose and impact of international justice.

[*Editor's Note: The audience watches a film about international justice.*]

So this short clip and this story that we're trying to tell, I hope it raises for you some of the hard questions about international justice today. What I want to do now is move to really specify some of those purposes. Why do we show these clips? In those ten minutes, I think you saw a bunch of different actors, and different ideas about what these courts should be doing. For example, what should these courts be doing and who is impacted by them, whether it is a soccer coach who lost eight members on his team in 1993 to 1994 or the woman who lost her son in a sniping during the war, or whether it is in some theoretical way, an assertion of laws or an assertion of values. Why do we have these tribunals, and what is their purpose?

I want to suggest a couple of different ways of thinking about the purposes of these tribunals. I will start, as it is always wise to start, with Hannah Arendt, who writes:

> The purpose of the trial is to render justice and nothing else. Even the noblest of ulterior purposes can only detract from the law's

main business: to weigh the charges brought against the accused, to render judgment, and to mete out due punishment.

In other words, Hannah Arendt, who spent almost a year in Israel during the Eichmann trial in the early 1960s, watched the entire trial, spoke with prosecutors and victims, and sought to understand what this trial was all about.

She comes away from it really worried. I urge people to go back and read *Eichmann in Jerusalem* (1963). If you haven't read it, or if you haven't read it in a long time, it is amazing how contemporary it feels because the questions are still so relevant. It is still about international justice, but it is about a domestic trial that took place in Israel. She sees that it is an affirmation or implementation of international rules in a domestic court, but that people on different sides of the question wanted this to be a trial. It was supposed to educate Israeli school children about what happened in the war, or it was supposed to educate the world about the Holocaust. It was supposed to be a trial that had these broader purposes of teaching. She didn't think that was worth it.

She thought at its root it was a trial about one person's guilt or innocence, and that was the only thing that the trial could be about. It might be for others, after the trial, to go through the material to try to make sense of it, and create a narrative, but once you go down the road of using the trial for some other purpose, in her view, you start to go down a path of making the trial look like a show trial rather than a real weighing of truth or guilt. From her perspective, we need to focus on the trial itself and ask ourselves if this person is guilty of these alleged crimes.

Now, fast forward to 1993 again. This is a picture (referring to a photograph in a PowerPoint presentation) of the United Nations Security Council. On May 26, 1993, the Security Council adopted the statute for the ICTY, for the Yugoslavian tribunal. In the course of adopting it, they said, here is what we're doing. It is always nice to know why some legislative body is doing something. Here they told you. I don't think it makes it any easier to understand which of these is more important than the others.

Among the purposes are: to put an end to such crimes and bring to justice the persons responsible for them, a straightforward concept of accountability that contributes to the restoration and maintenance of peace. Now, that might be a rhetorical element, but there is also an element here that indicates that, in order for the Security Council to act in a situation like this, it has to act under what is known as Chapter 7 of the United Nations Charter. In other words, the Security Council has to act as a measure of maintaining peace and security. So, it could be that this is just language, a reference to the Charter as a legal issue because in order for the Security Council to step into the situation in Bosnia they had to justify the action under this section of the Charter, they had to have a legal basis. But as you will see in a moment, some people took that pretty seriously, that creating a tribunal is also about bringing and restoring peace.

Finally, another purpose is to ensure that said violations are halted and effectively redressed. In addition to just having accountability, there is an element of deterrence. If we have these tribunals, if we have this particular tribunal, then maybe in the future, people will actually think twice about whether they should commit the crime. We're trying to deter people in Bosnia from committing a crime. Here in the Security Council we see a mixed sort of instrumental and symbolic reasons.

The instrumental reasons being deterrence — actually stopping people from committing a crime — and then, second, contributing to peace and reconciliation by having an actual role in bringing peace to the region.

Then there are expressive or symbolic purposes as well, like simple accountability. This isn't about some cost/benefit thing. This is an international community, we want to assert values and we want to hold people accountable. It is not really an instrumental thing, as more of this is what we do. So there is the assertion of values.

On top of all this at the time this is happening, there is also this ongoing question of whether this is simply an effort by the Security Council to show that we're doing something. It's as if it is saying, "We're not going to be able to stop the war, but we're going to set up this court to hold those accountable for its worst excesses."

Now this picture (referring to a photograph in a PowerPoint presentation) is Antonio Cassese. He is one of the leading figures in international criminal law. He is an Italian law professor. He was the first president and chief judge of the ICTY. This is at the time, so you have to put your mind into 1994. There were no defendants in The Hague. This is a court that exists more or less in theory. There are probably forty or fifty people who work there, and Judge Cassese is building this tribunal. He is essentially arguing that this tribunal has relevance. He said: "The role of the tribunal cannot be overemphasized. Far from being a vehicle for revenge, it is a tool for promoting reconciliation and restoring true peace."

We saw before that this element is in the Security Council's actual resolution adopting the statute, peace, and reconciliation. I don't mean to say that Cassese is this pie-in-the-sky jurist who thinks that law can solve everything; he is very much not. It's a very long report, so I am summarizing what is good from it. So he is not naive. But he says that the tribunal is about more than these other things; it's also about promoting reconciliation and serving as a tool for peace. This is early ICTY. The question is, how does it do that? How does it actually serve? It is holding people to account, but how does that serve to bring peace?

This was a particularly difficult question in 1994 when there may have been seventy people indicted and yet nobody was in the dock, and no defendants were being held at the Dutch prison near the beach in The Hague. It also doesn't answer the question, in the middle of the 1990s, posed by the mantra "there can be no peace without justice." It's still one of the core values of the international justice community and those who advocate for international justice. But what if justice conflicts with peace? Maybe it doesn't and that's what we can talk about. Maybe justice can always be a part of peacemaking, but it is how you do it. What if simply having a tribunal doesn't deter crimes, but what it might do, at least for those indicted, is encourage them to think, I can't lose this war now because, if I lose this war now, I am going to prison in The Hague. In thinking about the purpose of peace and justice and how those interrelate, we have to think about some of the impacts, some of the unintended consequences as well. That is early ICTY.

Then in another picture (referring to a photograph in a PowerPoint presentation), you see Judge Gabrielle Kirk McDonald, who was actually a federal district judge in Texas. She was the second president of the ICTY after Cassese when she went over to the tribunal. She was the first American judge to sit on the ICTY and presided over the first trial at

ICTY. This is in 1996, two years after Cassese says we are all about peace and reconciliation. She says something quite different. She says, and it should be taken in the context of a specific trial:

> Ensuring that this first trial will be conducted as fairly and as expeditiously as possible with justice being both done and being seen to be done. That's the main purpose regardless of all the apparent trappings of today.

That is its sole raison d'être; that is its only reason for being. Its only reason for being is to do justice in this particular case.

Separately she writes how it can't be about all these other things. It can't be about peace and reconciliation. Now there are other purposes that might be involved here. There are purposes of telling the narrative of what happened during the war. There are purposes about truth telling in general. Those are valid purposes, but what Judge McDonald and Hannah Arendt are suggesting, and even what some of the members of the Security Council are suggesting, is that, when we have an actual trial, the trial can only be about the guilt or innocence of the individual brought there.

As far as the whole tribunal is concerned, what are its purposes? Can it do these other things? Can it bring peace to a region? If it can, how does it do so? We can pick and choose among those cases, where, sometimes it might foster peace and sometimes it might not. Or, should we think of these international tribunals as we have them in domestic situations, where we have a federal prosecutor and he sees a crime, and in the idealized version of that, he goes after the criminal. Of course, prosecutors also have some discretion; they don't have to go after every criminal. That's a bit hard to figure out how that works on an international level. When Luis Moreno Ocampo, the chief prosecutor for the ICC, has these different cases in front of him, which one does he choose? Does he decide, in the case of Darfur, not to go after al-Bashir because of the impact it might have on the peace process or the impact it might have on individuals in refugee camps? Because al-Bashir might react by kicking out aid workers, as he did. Should that be a part of what he considers? In other words, should it be part of his consideration, when he's thinking about who to indict, whether it will move toward reconciliation, or actually undermine it.

Now, regardless of all these doubts I might be seeding for you, in terms of whether international justice works or what its purposes are meant to be, I want to end with this quote by Hannah Arendt: "If genocide is an actual possibility of the future, then no people on earth can feel reasonably sure of its continued existence without the help and protection of international law."

In other words, she has doubts about these tribunals. She doubts whether you can have a court or a trial that teaches people about crime or some conflict. Yet, she still believes that international law and the implementation of international law is crucial in the face of genocide, in the face of war crimes, and in the face of crimes against humanity. There is no question about that, and I don't question that at all. The only question is whether these tribunals serve those purposes.

As we're moving forward in international justice, it is easy to see that the last fifteen years where you have international courts from Bosnia, Rwanda, Cambodia, Sierra Leone, and now the International Criminal Court, which is in some ways a kind of middle Africa kind of court at the moment. You can look at that and say that, today, international criminal law is a major player in international politics. In part, that's true, but I think what General Clark said is also true. I don't think it is irreversible. In other words, the ICTY and the ICTR, the Yugoslavian and Rwandan tribunals, are going to shut down in the next few years. The International Criminal Court has several cases, but, in a lot of ways it is struggling: struggling with its leadership and struggling to see whether it can get somebody like al-Bashir. In other ways, however, international criminal justice is also sprinting, I mean, it is becoming more about ICC. It puts a lot of weight on the shoulders of Ocampo and others in the The Hague. It is unclear if it is going to work, but I think, in order for it to work, we need to know what it is we want it to do. I hope this will be an opportunity to think about these courts, and decide whether you think they are effective and what you think they should be doing.

May 16, 2009
SGI-USA Santa Monica Culture of Peace Resource Center

NOTE:

1. Karadžic's trial began in October 2009. The Hague indictment charges Karadzic with genocide, complicity in genocide, liquidation, murder, punishment, deportation, inhumane acts, and other crimes committed against Muslims, Croats, and other civilians like non-Serbs in Bosnia-Herzegovina during the war in that former Yugoslav republic. The Hague Tribunal is expected to pass its first-instance verdict in December 2015.

Striving to Create the Will to Peace

James Lawson

Nonviolence Strategist
United States Civil Rights Movement

James M. Lawson Jr. is a minister, university professor, and civil rights activist. He was a leading theoretician and tactician of nonviolence within the American Civil Rights Movement.

As a college student, he joined the Fellowship for Reconciliation and the Congress of Racial Equality. He declared himself a conscientious objector and refused to report for the draft in 1951, serving fourteen months in prison as a result. As a Methodist missionary to India, he studied Gandhi's principles of nonviolence. Enrolling in the Vanderbilt University Divinity School, he began nonviolence training workshops for the Southern Christian Leadership Conference. These led to the sit-ins in downtown Nashville in 1960. He played a role in efforts such as the Freedom Rides and the Mississippi Freedom Project (Freedom Summer).

He was expelled from Vanderbilt because of his civil rights activities. He became pastor of Centenary Methodist Church in Memphis, and in 1968 was chair of the strategy committee for a strike by African American sanitation workers. He invited Martin Luther King Jr. to come to Memphis to support the strike. Reverend King delivered his famous "Mountaintop" speech there the day before he was assassinated.

Reverend Lawson continued his ministry, leading Holman Methodist Church in Los Angeles from 1974 to 1999, as well as his social activism and nonviolence training. Vanderbilt apologized to Lawson for expelling him, and he later served as a Distinguished Visiting Professor at the school.

In 2004, he received the Community of Christ International Peace Award.

James Lawson speaks compellingly of many topics included in the eight action areas defined in the 1999 United Nations Declaration and Programme of Action on a Culture of Peace, particularly the first, fostering a culture of peace through education, and the eighth, promoting international peace and security.

His talk focused on outlining the means of refocusing

America's resources toward contributing to peace,
beginning with individual efforts. Reverend Lawson told
the audience that, especially in light of a shared global
history of nonstop conflict since 1945, "billions of ordinary
men and women do want peace." He shared that "we hold
in our hands and hearts the key to making the will to peace
vanquish the powers that dictate and dominate the mind
and practice of our nation."

I want to talk about this business of the will to peace. I hope at the same
time that I may say something that will provoke you and be quite con-
troversial to you, but that will also be helpful. I think that, in our land
today, although we have lots of controversies, in my judgment many of
them are more connected to an anemic kind of intellectual and spiritual life than to the robust issues of faith or practice or justice or peace.

The first point I want to make is that there is no will for peace in the
United States and in much of the world in which we live. There is instead
a massive will to dominate and control, to manage conflict through violence and threats. There are huge expenditures on the military forces
of violence, the technologies of war and for war. War and violence have
become a major means to transfer money from 90 percent of the population of the world to the top 10 percent. This is very acute in much of
the Western world. The world forces that have dominated the earth for
the last five hundred years continue to dominate today and, through
the United States in particular, are on the side of conflict and division.
Those forces *will* not for peace but *will* for power and wealth and violence by any means necessary. When the language of peace is used in a
large swath of the world, that language is really more about animosity,
war, and injustice. It is much less about what many of us in this room
would consider peace.

A major force of what I am calling righteous evil today is what I
call "plantation capitalism." It is largely influenced by the fact that the

United States in the last one hundred years and colonialism for the last five hundred years turned the unknown world into a plantation for Western Europe, Western culture, and Western economic gain. At the heart of plantation capitalism was the notion that workers were property, not human beings, and did not deserve to reap the benefit of their labor. The major recipient of that stance is the United States more than any other country, and for the last 109 years, we have financed that stance more than any other country. The militarization of the last sixty years has certainly compounded our belief in the efficacy of violence, but these four factors — genocide, racism, sexism, plantation capitalism — are all part of it. These forces have welded the culture of violence. For example, we have more than 800 military installations in 130 countries; our annual expenditures for this purpose are now being acknowledged as 800 billion dollars a year, probably a trillion dollars a year. We are increasing those expenditures daily in places like Africa, Central Asia, Iraq, and Afghanistan.

I am pushing hard on this simple thesis that there is no will for peace among many of the world's powers. Too many religious people want wars and rumors of wars. We have these startling religious notions that the more calamity and chaos, the better it is. Too many of us want rumors of war and chaos, yet let me make a major footnote at this point. It is my contention that billions of ordinary men and women around the world do, in fact, want peace. They are weary of the conflicts, of the tensions, of the pains, of the calamities, whether in Zaire, Liberia, Iran, or Afghanistan, or wherever. There are people in Los Angeles and probably every major city of the world who agonize and grieve for peace. Ordinary men and women around the world would like to be able to concentrate on the issues they think are most critical, namely, caring for their families, sustaining their livelihood, and putting bread and food on their tables and having shelter, and the possibilities of influencing the well-being and the education of their children; being able to participate in their villages and their neighborhoods, in their immediate environments in a stable and inspiring fashion that can allow them to certify hope for themselves and for their children. Literally billions of ordinary men and women do want peace, but I want to maintain that many of the powers and forces that be make huge expenditures of money and energy to channel their will into violence and war.

I am going to say very clearly, as clearly as I can, that the difficulties in our world do not rest with billions of people, no matter what their responsibilities may be. They rest with the principalities and powers, to use a notion from the Apostle Paul in chapter six of Ephesians.[1] The conflict and turmoil in our world in large measure rests upon the principalities and powers, which very often we will not identify among ourselves, or in our own religions, or in our own nations. This may be a painful thing for us to see, and I understand that, and it grieves me as well to make this kind of statement, but I believe the major influence in the twentieth century and the twenty-first century on the side of conflict and war is our own United States of America.

The United States is the primary leader instigating and launching this violence. In the twentieth century we did it in more than forty countries. If you go into an almanac and do a little survey, there are a number of these outlined in books now, especially in the last ten to fifteen years. If you just do a survey of the nations where we've sent a battleship up the rivers, where we have bombed, or where we have sent in the Marines, or where we have financed freedom fighters, or where we have had our own covert government undermine an election or leave behind forces to undermine the possibility of an election, you can list the names of these countries without any difficulty. I want to say then that we of the religions and we the peoples who urgently talk about peace and claim peace as a value have failed. Since 1945 the earth has seen an almost endless flow of blood. In many of those cases, if the United States has not been an overt participant, it has been a covert participant, and it has armed all sides, not both sides, but all sides, in many different conflicts in my own lifetime since 1945.

The point I want to drive home to this group, my fellow citizens, is that there is no way toward developing a will to peace as long as we, the wealthiest nation, deceives itself about our policies and practices around the world. As long as we have covert government agencies that operate for the domination of life rather than for the liberation of life, as long as we substitute a cold war with the war against terrorism and we call all our opponents in the world "evil," as long as we spend so much of our resources, both human and financial, and scheme on the side of conflicts rather than on the side of the struggle for truth and wonder, the will to peace is a long way off. As long as we have a government more interested in the domination of life than in the liberation of life, business institutions more interested in accumulating wealth and power than in emulating the ancient human visions of the earth as fully dedicated to healing and in bettering and enlarging life, we remain in trouble. I myself am still persuaded that we are not out of the woods at all because our intentions are not wrapped up in our words, our intentions are wrapped up in how we spend our money or how we organize ourselves and others for today and tomorrow.

The second point I wish to make is this: There is no will to peace, but we can discover a will to peace. When I use the term *peace*, I am not talking about some kind of acquiescence or apathy; I don't think that you can be a wide-awake human being in our world, or a religionist of any kind in our world, and consider peace a primary category of the religious life. My own spiritual journey has seen me maladjusted and uneasy at almost every decade of my life. Although I have lived a life in which I essentially have never gone without food or a suit of clothing unless I deliberately went on a fast. Nevertheless, my life has been persistently uneasy, not for myself or even for my own family, but uneasy about a great variety of people whose lives are daily devastated by the circumstances we built into this twenty-first century. In spite of that, I want to insist that we can discover the will to peace and the urgency to peace.

I want to outline very briefly, four major points. First of all I want to commend the work of Mohandas Karamchand Gandhi. In his many experiments with nonviolence and his codifying of nonviolence, he insists that the first step in looking at a scene is to investigate, study, examine, explore, and look at it from many different angles, and find out all that can be found out about it. I would like to suggest that as an ongoing step to explore the human situation beginning with ourselves in our own nation. I would dare to suggest that, no matter our religious perspectives, by and large we are more shaped by the spirituality of racism, sexism, violence, and greed than we are by the ancient wisdom of the human race concerning the impulses of peace. I would lift that up as a primary examination of our plight in this wonderful land and the more than three hundred million people who call ourselves residents and citizens and comrades in this nation. We are more shaped by the -isms out of our past than we are by our proclamations of faith.

I want to boost the notion that to be aware of ourselves as a people is to be aware of the fact that our history is quite unique in so many different ways. This is a nation that formed itself by essentially taking the land from the ten to fifteen million indigenous people who were on these contiguous states. We took the land and we justified the taking of the land and relegated those people to reservations and to the poorest demographics of our people, and we say nothing about it and do literally nothing about it.

I believe along with people like Frederick Douglass and James Baldwin that our past is not a dead thing; it is a living thing because we carry on the vibrations as well as many of the attitudes of the past with us into the present moment. That is the beginning of our racism because we define the Native Americans as being less than human; we define them as being the other. We documented that with 250 years of the slavery of a people from Africa, where we made the theology of racism a creed, a lifestyle, and an economic understanding that we have not yet disavowed.

From the beginning of our nation we insisted that women were second-class citizens, less than equal, that they did not have the right to vote. We often had laws across our history where women could not do certain things in terms of education and the rest of it. That lives on today. It lives on today in denominations in the Protestant world where it's insisted on principle that a woman must be submissive to the man. It is current theology that comes out of our past to beat up on us. All of these forces that I have mentioned from our own past were undergirded by violence — the violence of speech, the violence of attitudes, and the violence of the fist and the club and the bomb. It is these forces that, in my judgment, have more to do with the shaping of American policy in the world than anything else.

We must face the reality that for much of the last sixty years we have had a bipartisan policy that has seen the world as a dangerous place to live in, not as a world filled with people like ourselves, and not as the given of life and the given of grace by the creator. It is my simple contention that we must look deeply and heartedly at ourselves and our policies. I don't pretend that you and I in this room are necessarily individually responsible for these; we have in many ways inherited them, but they are clearly a part of the path that we must examine. As we do this, I think that we will see the other side of the coin, the other lining, that this will to peace on the part of billions of people can be exploited, because as a people in this land we have become a more activist people than I have ever known us to be in a great variety of ways. If we use the Gandhian approach to investigate and discover the human plight, it will liberate us for self-examination and for looking at where there might be places where change can take place.

Second, I want to suggest that out of that investigation we can find and celebrate the human family. I like what the Interfaith Communities United for Justice and Peace have said, across the last five years especially, that religion must stop blessing war and violence. I like to say it another way. Religions of the world and the people of religion must stop blessing war and violence in their many masks. The human family is that to which we must learn to belong. I rejoice in my own particularities as a man, as a black man, but I know that my particularities, race, Christianity, point at me and transform my life to belonging to all humankind and to having human affections for all — none are excluded. I think that it has come out of the fact personally, that as I have wrestled with the business of racism in particular, I have recognized that the opposite of racism is to discover the deep streams of what life is about in your own bones and in your own DNA.

In many ways, many of the leaders of institutions in the United States do not have the will for peace because they have disconnected themselves from the human family. I think, for, example, of the long years of the Cold War being repeated now in the wars with Iraq and Afghanistan and against South Korea and North Korea. My government, supported by too many governors and too many state legislatures as well, between 1945 and 1990, never saw world leaders in Africa, Asia, and Latin America, very often even in Europe, as being competent human beings who had something to offer the world and to offer us as a nation. I cannot get out of my mind the fact that, in the 1980s Nelson Mandela, now considered one of the outstanding human beings of our time, was called a communist in the United States and, by national leaders, as someone who deserved to be hung by the apartheid government. The whole presence changed in South Africa with the African National Congress, nearly one hundred years old now. It was dismissed as entirely irresponsible and unable to make any sort of decisions that we in the United States could call human, just, and fair, to add to our own understanding of the world. We need to rediscover that the human race is indeed God's, the Creator's great remarkable gift to us. We need to discover out of our own history, the energy and the right to reclaim it.

The third point I wish to make is that, on as many levels as possible, we must organize campaigns and movements nonviolently for equality, liberty, and justice on every kind of issue. The period of agitation and protest in the early part of the eighteenth century prior to 1776, the Declaration of Independence and the like, is what in many ways in our own land prepared the soil for many ordinary men and women to recognize and, in a time of tyranny, dare to launch an experiment of self-governance. We need a time in the twenty-first century, now where similar kinds of protests and agitation against a great variety of wrongs in our own time are pushing for genuine equality, liberty, and justice, when we can help to prepare the soil for the shift of our nation toward democracy.

The part of that I want to insist upon is that you and I so often are bound by so many ties with plantation capitalism and the powers that be in our country, that these hammer away at us every day, making us feel that domestic issues are unimportant, and that Iraq and the Middle East, Afghanistan are where the priorities are for peace. I see this as one of the major failures of many of us who are peaceniks, that we agree with the covert forces in the United States. The well-being of the people of our land is secondary to our expanded democracy in Iraq and Iran and elsewhere. Then, in fact, when the Bush Administration sets up the African Command to build military installations along the East Coast of Africa, along that huge ocean line, they are insisting to us that structural poverty is unimportant, and that the well-being of all the children in our land is very secondary. We can only rediscover our will to peace out of making practical the things that we claim about ourselves.

The fourth point: Let those of us in religion—whether Buddhist, Christian, Jewish, or Islamic—strive to direct campaigns to dismantle injustice, hunger, structural poverty, domestic violence, and the like in our own midst. I like what the National Women's Party did in 1914. This group of women said to the major suffrage organizations: "We will not support World War I because we think the issue is in the United States. The right of women to vote is the major battle for democracy in the United States, not the war in Europe." They did something rather spectacular. They demonstrated in front of the White House six days a week, and they did this for almost a year, in which they said, essentially,

"President Wilson come home, this is where the struggle for democracy is." They took huge cans, empty steel cans, and they burned his speeches in those steel cans on the sidewalk in front of the White House, proclaiming with their signs that the most serious struggle for truth is over here, not over there.

I would like to suggest that that is one of the models we can use for agitation and protest in the United States. As that work really gains passion and zeal in the United States, we will see the will for peace emerge. We will see the way to peace emerge as well. This has been said much better by Pope John Paul, when he said the way to peace is to do justice.

Then my fifth point is simply this: Let each of us become a majority of one. I may not have very much control over what Congress can do, I have no control, but I have control over what I will stand for and live for, how I will do my work and how I will live. I may not have any kind of power over the forces of sexism and structural poverty in our country, but I can at least identify myself with a different kind of society. Although it is not an easy thing, it is complicated, because we are all connected to one another. When we pay taxes, when we live in this country, we are all in some way murderers of people in Iraq and elsewhere, because it's our land and we cannot cleanse ourselves in that fashion. We can nonetheless, without arrogance and without personal tyranny, insist that "I will be a majority of one for compassion and truth, for hope and dignity, and that no man, no woman, or any child of any kind will be stranger to me. I will live my life seeking to be a part of the great stream of human wisdom and hope." Each one of us can engage in the ministry of the discipline, if you will, of one-on-one in our own families, among our own friends, among our neighbors, to help build in that most intimate community where we are, where we live, and build into that intimate community the sense of the beloved community that is itself a sign and a symbol of the beloved world for all humankind that we seek, and see that work in that essential circle of life, in every way that's possible.

Gandhi suggested that part of the nonviolent methodology is to build it within your intimate kinships, your extended family. Help that family to be a part of the larger golden purpose and task of willing peace and willing truth. The will to peace is available as a gift of life itself. We must say no to violence and war and to the military preparations that produce war, no to any share of our taxes that go for hurting rather than for healing. We can say yes to creating a society where all our babies and all our children and all our young people become the priority of our public budgets. How shameful it is that we are arguing all over the country and that the first things being cut are the things that belong to what we bequeath and provide for our children and for the people who are vulnerable. Shameful! Already the forces of hurt exist — nuclear weapons and the devastation that they perform, much of it invisible to too many of us. The will for peace, the soil for peace, must precede the way to peace.

I would urge all of us to simply see that, in the mundane things that we seek to do day after day, in the building of the community where we live, work, and play, we hold in our hands and hearts the key for making the will to peace vanquish the powers that dictate and dominate the mind and practice of our nation. I am personally persuaded that the will of the universe, the will of the Creator, is humankind, healing humankind solving our issues in a fashion that builds confidence in all of us for tomorrow, looking at things as they are, expecting that they can become what they must become, so that we human beings can begin to tap the larger possibilities of life itself. I refuse to believe that the best of this nation or our earth is in the past. I believe that we have not yet tapped the infinite possibilities for life, for justice, for truth, for the human family to overcome the issues of the powers that be and to create new powers that can mean truth and hope.

June 20, 2009
SGI-USA Santa Monica Culture of Peace Resource Center

NOTE:

1. "For our struggle is not with flesh and blood but with the principalities, with the powers, with the world rulers of this present darkness, with the evil spirits in the heavens." See http://www.usccb.org/bible/ephesians/6.

¡Si Se Puede! Yes We Can!

Julie Chávez Rodriguez

Programs Director, César E. Chávez Foundation

Julie Chávez Rodriguez is the granddaughter of labor and civil rights activist César Chávez and programs director for the César E. Chávez Foundation, a nonprofit charitable organization, founded in 1993 by César's family and friends to educate people about his life and work and to engage all, particularly youth, to carry on his values and timeless vision for a better, more just world.

At a young age, Ms. Rodriguez was exposed to the working people's struggle at the United Farm Workers' (UFW) headquarters at La Paz, located in Keene, California. She began volunteering with the UFW at five years old. Since then, she has energized La Causa, the movement to advance farm workers' rights, through campaigns and other events. Ms. Rodriguez supports service-learning projects by leading the César E. Chávez Foundation's "Educating the Heart" school program and participating as a fellow in National Service-Learning Emerging Leaders Initiative, the National Service-Learning Partnership, and the National Youth Leadership Council.

Julie graduated from the University of California, Berkeley, with a bachelor of arts in Latin American Studies. Throughout her four years at UC Berkeley she was a member of the Farm Worker Support Committee, among other organizations. In addition, she coordinated guest lecturers who spoke about farm worker issues, supported campus campaigns to reinstate Affirmative Action, and advocated for bilingual education to provide youth with increased educational opportunities. During the summers, Julie worked full time for the AFL-CIO's Union Summer Program, where she coordinated and administered internships for students across the nation.

She has vast experience developing curricular materials in collaboration with educators, researchers, and civic leaders, in addition to conducting professional development workshops for educators across the country.

Annually, Ms. Rodriguez is invited to guest lecture at colleges and universities to share the relevance of her grandfather's legacy to today's social issues. Like her grandfather, Julie believes that "the end of all education should surely be service to others. '

Julie Rodriguez addresses several of the eight action areas defined in the 1999 United Nations Declaration and Programme of Action on a Culture of Peace, most notably the first, fostering a culture of peace through education, and the seventh, supporting participatory communication and the free flow of information and knowledge.

She says: "That is what I see as my work today, working with young people and engaging them. This concept of education of the heart is not just in words and not just in theory, but most important, through their own actions and service to their community. I found service to be a very transforming experience, in particular for young people who are in the process of exploring themselves, their relationships with one another, and their relationship with the world. It is a strong foundation that I know I was given as a young child, and I think all of our young people deserve, and that's the opportunity to experience our own gifts and talents, our own ability to make a change, however small that change might seem."

I was not aware I was going to be receiving an award today so I feel a little caught off guard, but obviously am very humbled in particular about the words inscribed on the award. We just finished a conversation with another group and I believe opportunities like these are always powerful learning and growing experiences.

Speaking of personal transformation, often I have found myself doing internal transformation and realizing that it is only one part of the process. The other part is coming together in a community like we are doing today to dialogue, articulate, and share that vision with one another. As Mahatma Gandhi once said, "Transformation happens when one person's vision becomes that of many." Hopefully our conversation today will enable all of us to join together in community while physically here, but also as we move to our weekend and week, and through the rest of this year.

I want to read a poem my grandfather wrote that allows me to reflect on who he was as a person and some of his values and principles that transcend his own time on this earth. The poem is actually a prayer. I talk about it as a poem because I work with K–12 schools, and you can't talk about prayer in school. It was originally written as a prayer. It's called "The Prayer of the Farm Worker's Struggle."

PRAYER OF THE FARM WORKER'S STRUGGLE

Show me the suffering of the most miserable;
So I will know my people's plight.

Free me to pray for others;
For you are present in every person.

Help me take responsibility for my own life;
So that I can be free at last.

Grant me courage to serve others;
For in service there is true life.

Give me honesty and patience;
So that I can work with other workers.

Bring forth song and celebration;
So that the Spirit will be alive among us.

Let the Spirit flourish and grow;
So that we will never tire of the struggle.

Let us remember those who have died for justice;
For they have given us life.

Help us love even those who hate us;
So that we can change the world.

When I listen to the poem and oftentimes reflect on it, I see certain elements that stand true to my life and to where I am at. At different points in my day or in my week, there are particular elements that are stronger than others. I think that "Help us love even those who hate us" emanates with me when I am stuck in traffic and maybe want to ram the car next to me that's not cooperating. I think it's important that we think about how my grandfather's life and words transcend his own experience and existence.

I want to share who he was, his life and work and the Farm Worker Movement. I think it is important, as we look back on history, to see people like my grandfather, ordinary people who found themselves in extraordinary times, confronting extraordinary challenges and having extraordinary opportunities. Too often when we look back on history we tend to glorify the realities in which these people existed. Like my grandfather, sometimes we look back and assume that all the farm workers were ready to be organized and were excited about it, and that it was something they wanted to do. That wasn't the reality, like many of the struggles and issues we face today.

I want to begin by showing a baby picture of my grandfather (referring to a photograph in a PowerPoint presentation) because, like most individuals who have made an impact on our communities, on our world, or on our lives, they weren't born leaders, they weren't born ready to take on that task, and they weren't born already knowing what impact they were going to make. They were innocent and they were children. It's usually through their experiences, their preparation, their mentors, and through their lifetime that they are given the opportunity to develop the skills, talents, and abilities to make that change.

My grandfather had only an eighth-grade education. Some folks don't realize that. He wasn't formally educated beyond the eighth grade because he had to work full time in the fields picking fruits and vegetables to support his family. This is actually a photo (referring to a photograph in a PowerPoint presentation) of his eighth-grade graduation. He really loved education, but not so much school. He had some traumatic experiences in school. As a young child, one time he was forced to wear a sign that said, "I am a clown, I speak Spanish," because he used Spanish in the classroom. That's questionable today, but if you can imagine it, in the 1930s and 1940s it just wasn't allowed. His experience in school wasn't all that great, but for him education went beyond the classroom.

It was a lifelong practice. He was an avid reader and saw the opportunity for knowledge to translate into power; he saw education as a vehicle, as an opportunity for him to gain the knowledge he needed to take meaningful action as it related to the farm workers.

My grandfather married my grandmother, Helen Fabela Chávez, in 1948 after he returned from serving in the Navy in World War II. My grandmother played a critical role in his lifetime; she was his backbone in a lot of ways. He ended up cleaning docks most of the time, which was more suitable to his character. It wasn't really one of combat as we see later on in his lifetime. There is this beautiful card we came across after he passed away that was in his desk. It was a note to my grandmother saying how much he appreciated her courage and sacrifice and strength over the years, because he couldn't have accomplished what he did without her. For him to not only know that but articulate and express it was a powerful voice for my grandmother.

As much as she was in her home, caring for and nurturing the children, she was also on the front lines of the strikes and picket lines, and as I have sometimes shared, sometimes lying on railroad tracks to stop grapes from being shipped out from the Central Valley to other areas of the state. To see in them a connection that wasn't just a husband and wife relationship, but a partnership and a level of mentorship both of them experienced with one another was, for me, beautiful to witness as a child, and enabled me to learn more about them as an adult and embrace.

My grandparents had eight children, and my mother was one of their eight children. Family played a critical role in the Farm Worker Movement and in my grandfather's life's work. The expectation was never that this was a cause he was going to champion alone, but a movement of people who were not just going to transform the conditions they were working in, but also transform the communities in which they lived and of which they were a part. His family became a very critical piece of that, and in fact, sometimes the only way they could spend time together as a family was on picket lines, strikes, and marches.

A cousin of mine has a joke she often says, that we didn't go on family picnics, we went on family pickets. That was a common outing for us. Rather than be on the beach in Santa Monica, we would stand in front of the Vons Supermarket telling people not to buy grapes. At least we were still out in the sun.

For my grandfather, again, having his family be a part of this and then creating an extended family and community with the farm workers he served, was very much a part of his belief in developing the capacity of people. He believed that each one of us has the potential to change our own lives and the communities in which we live. He saw that potential not just in himself but in his children, in his wife, and in each and every farm worker he came into contact with. Despite and against previous odds, he held the faith and the belief in people and accomplished what no one else could ever achieve—he was able to get people to see that they had this potential.

Part of how he learned, or I guess his introduction to understanding how people could realize their personal potential and realize the potential they had as a collective community, was working with the Community Service Organization. This came about because of his first and what I say was his most important mentor, a Catholic priest named Father Donald McDonnell, who was overseeing a parish in San Jose in a community called Sal Si Puedes, which means, "get out if you can." You can imagine the conditions in this community. I don't know that any of us would want to live in a community where the archway, as you drive into it, says ... "Get Out If You Can."

That's not the vision or the ideal each one of us had, but that's where my grandfather was living, and he found a lot of support and connection with this Catholic priest. He would oftentimes go to Father McDonnell to share his frustrations and anger with him. He saw the conditions of the community in Sal Si Puedes; they didn't have streetlights, there wasn't adequate running water, and they didn't have sidewalks. When it would rain, the community would flood and there was no way of dealing with that. He was upset and angry and Father McDonnell saw in him the beginning of someone who could initiate and inspire the kind of change Father McDonnell knew was critically important to Sal Si Puedes.

Father McDonnell gave him *The Principles of Nonviolence* by Mahatma Gandhi. My grandfather read that and saw such a powerful tool in this concept of nonviolent resistance, of people coming together to demand a better future, a better reality. He saw a great potential in what Mahatma

Gandhi had realized in India. Around this time a community organizer named Fred Ross came into the Sal Si Puedes area and, in true community organizer fashion, Fred asked what institutions in this community he could go to that would help him identify critical leaders. He knew the Catholic Church was strong and had a strong following from this community, so he went to Father McDonnell and said: "Father McDonnell, I need someone in this community who cares about the issues and conditions and is willing to stand up and do something about it. He doesn't have to have a lot of experience or education, just be someone who cares and wants to do something about it." Father McDonnell said, "I have the person for you."

Father McDonnell gave Fred my grandfather's name and address. Having grown up in farm worker communities throughout his life, my grandfather wasn't experienced in dealing and working with people known as outsiders. The community of Sal Si Puedes, situated in San Jose, was in close proximity to the University of California, Berkeley, and too often, folks came into Sal Si Puedes ostensibly to help the poor farm workers or poor Mexicans, but actually came to study them. They would ask, "What do Mexicans eat?" … and, "Why do beans have so much nutrition and how can you use corn so many ways?"

My grandfather grew very distrustful of people from outside the community who came in to help the farm workers. When Fred came to his door, he wouldn't allow him in, and he kept telling my grandmother that she had to lie for him. My grandfather said, "Ah, tell him I'm not home, and I don't want to talk to him; he is just going to ask me a bunch of questions and go back to his fancy old house." That was the perception he had. Finally my grandmother, being the strong woman that she was, decided she wasn't going to take it anymore. She said: "You know what, you do your own dirty work. You lie for yourself. I am not taking it anymore. Next time he comes, you're going to have to deal with him." So he came, and, since this was before my grandfather practiced non-violence, he had plotted with his friends to invite him in and offer him a drink. He was also a smoker at the time, and they decided that, when he switched his cigarette from his right hand to his left, his friends were going to jump him to show Fred not to mess with our community.

He invited Fred in and Fred began talking about the ways that other communities similar to Sal Si Puedes had come together and started organizing themselves. They had made achieved strong victories, had gotten streetlights in their community, and now had regular sanitation pickups so the trash wasn't spread all over. Some of them had even gotten sidewalks. As my grandfather listened to Fred, he distinctly heard how people could come together and change their own lives and conditions, and even more so, how poor people could build power by organizing. It was so clear that he could almost taste it. He never switched the cigarette from his right hand to his left hand. His friends got antsy, and they were saying, come on, what's the plan, do you remember the plan? He was no longer subject to that plan. He no longer saw Fred as the same as many other people he had met. Finally, here was someone who wasn't there to tell them what to do or to tell them what they needed and what they should care about, but someone who wanted to listen and support and develop them to address their own needs, and transform their own community.

From that day forward, my grandfather worked as a community organizer with the Community Service Organization. That was the organization Fred had worked with. For those of you familiar with community organizing, it was an outgrowth of Saul Alinsky's work in Chicago, and came from that tradition of community organizing. The *Rules for Radicals* was a staple in every household; it almost became scripture in some ways for the Farm Worker Movement. During his ten years with the CSO he was trained as an organizer as he worked alongside his mentor, Fred Ross, day in and day out. Before that, my grandfather had no idea what it meant to register voters or even go out and speak publicly about an issue, or bring people together and get them to decide on an issue they wanted to build a campaign around.

Within the ten years that he practiced those skills, he realized that he really had this talent, this gift, this something of value he could offer to others or bring to others in a way that was an extension of the early teachings his mother had bestowed on him. Oftentimes they were in the framework of Catholic teachings, but they were about social justice, nonviolence, and bringing people together to transcend their realities. It's unfortunate that, too often in the conversation that happens around individuals, whether it's my grandfather or Dr. Martin Luther King Jr. or

Rosa Parks or many of the other civil rights leaders who have impacted our community, we start with the point when they chose to take action or they chose to stand up and fight back, but we don't look at the preparation that brought them to that point. We don't look at the individuals that influenced, mentored, and supported them. That's why I think it's important in particular to think about my grandfather's time in the Community Service Organization. Had he not been given the opportunity to think and practice and identify and refine his skills and talents, he would not have been prepared to go out and fight for the rights of farm workers in the way he did.

And as we think about the preparation and support all of us need, it's almost crazy to talk about history in a way that is void of that conversation or that real focus. I think we are doing a disservice to our young people if we give them the expectation that they are going to have to be born ready to take on the world, or that they are born as leaders, or that they already know what it is they are going to do, rather than give them opportunities to develop that potential over time. That's what sets my grandfather apart from others. He wasn't special; he wasn't born with a silver spoon in his mouth. He wasn't even the best speaker. Those of you who have heard his speeches know he wasn't like Dr. King; he wasn't eloquent and beautiful. He didn't necessarily have the ring that touches your soul the way you hear from folks like Dr. King.

What he did have was passion and an undying determination to change the lives of those who were closest to his own experience. That's why working with the CSO for ten years became, again, the preparation he needed to do what he saw as his calling and mission in life, and that was to change the conditions of farm workers. He talked about the fact that all farm workers share this common experience of humiliation. He talked about it in that way, not because he saw the work farm workers did as humiliating; if anything, it was the exact opposite. He saw it as the most critically important job and role that folks could perform. When we think about the fact that we enjoy food every day, and that we need food to sustain ourselves, to live and breathe, then we understand that those who bring food, the human hands that bring food to our tables, are treated so horribly — that is the humiliation he wanted to bring attention to. In many cultures and religions, oftentimes, food is seen as sacred, and if those who bring that sacred gift are treated like animals, or some-times are treated as if they are part of a production cycle, that is what he wanted to change.

Some folks obviously see him as a revolutionary or as someone who wanted to overthrow a farm labor system that made billions and bil-lions of dollars. That was part of the mission, but at the core, it was really about dignity and respect in humanity for the farm workers. If we can't treat these farm workers as individuals, and as a society, if we can't cre-ate that sense of connection with those who pick our food, then we are in a dangerous place. For him, it was about bringing that human face to the farm worker, to say that food doesn't magically appear in our gro-cery stores or in our homes or in our restaurants, but that there is sweat, tears, and sacrifice, and unfortunately today, sometimes death is a part of that process.

For him, going back and organizing farm workers was a natural next step. Although he enjoyed his work with the Community Service Orga-nization, he knew his fight was not in the urban centers in the state but in the fields with those whose experience he shared. After being away for ten years and not working in the fields, he realized anew that he had now experienced a level of disconnection. In a certain respect, he can maybe even be seen by some as that outsider coming in to help the farm workers, even though he had gone through that same experience. He was very careful not to recreate a system of oppression that he had seen and experienced, but instead one that was about empowering and building the indigenous leadership of farm workers to transform their own lives and realities. He knew this wasn't something that could just be imposed upon the workers, but that they had to reach a point where they understood and realized it wasn't that the growers were so power-ful, but that the workers had given up their power. That became a core component of the Farm Worker Movement and of his organizing efforts. It was not just getting the farm workers to realize and understand their own personal power, but even the organizers and those within the Farm Worker Movement.

I am a clear and direct product of that. I was given opportunities as a young person to exercise my own leadership and explore my own skills and talents and formulate my own understanding of what justice meant to me, of what humanity looked like. I was fortunate that I got to do this in the context of the Farm Worker Movement. I was one that wasn't solely focused on the farm workers, but I think one that began to translate out.

We saw the impact his life and work had on other prominent figures and other arenas and stages. This photo (referring to a photograph in a PowerPoint presentation) is of Dolores Huerta and Robert Kennedy. Dolores was the cofounder of the Farm Worker Movement. To me, Dolores is one of the strongest women activists I have ever known or learned or read about. This was from a time when women leadership wasn't common, especially in the labor movement. She was a teacher who worked in Stockton and was also mentored by Fred Ross, who had again sought out my grandfather. She became a strong and powerful female leader and role model for so many of us.

In talking about what that change was for her, what that transformational or transitional point was for her, Dolores said she went into class one day as a teacher and realized her role was not to teach these children who were too hungry to learn, but her role was to go out and make sure these children had food on their table every night. That's when she began to organize farm workers and that's when she began to create that change. I mentioned that Senator Robert Kennedy was there and that resulted in the attention that took the issue of farm workers and farm workers' rights from a small town in Delano, California, out to the nation, out to the national public. Senator Kennedy became an early supporter and advocate for farm workers' rights, first by actually commissioning a hearing and getting folks to expose what it was that farm workers were facing. Sometimes it's hard to imagine, but they didn't have restrooms in the fields. Just think about the sanitary issues related to that. Nowadays we're dealing with so many food safety and security issues, whether it's peanuts or spinach or other foods we're consuming, where sanitation and a just food system and other issues regarding our overall food system have become things we need to address.

Since they didn't have restrooms in the fields, they were often forced to go behind trees or in bushes, and you can imagine the difficulty for women in particular. They were also very segregated. In the 1960s, the face of farm workers looked very different than the face of farm

workers today. Today, about 80 percent of farm workers are undoc-
umented workers, mostly from Mexico. In the 1960s, you had Mex-
ican farm workers and a huge contingent of Filipino farm workers.
Some farm workers were leftover dust bowlers from Oklahoma. African American farm workers were still working in the fields, there was
even a contingent of Arab farm workers. One of the early martyrs of the
Farm Worker Movement was a gentleman by the name of Naji Daiful-
lah, who was unfortunately killed by a Kern County Sheriff. He was hit
in the back of the head by a billy club and dragged through the town of
Delano almost as an example of what could happen if you stood up and
fought for your rights.

It became a much broader and more widespread movement. It actually became a coalition of people coming together across racial and ethnic lines to identify as workers, to see their common connection and
common oppression as farm workers. Those from the public and in
leadership positions like Senator Kennedy realized their responsibility
in all of this, and realized that each one of us has a responsibility relat-
ing to the food we consume, even to other purchasing choices we make,
and we all have a responsibility to do right by one another and by our
communities.

My grandfather believed deeply in the concept and the notion of non-
violence; it wasn't just a political and tactical thing but was at the core
of who he was. This next picture (referring to a photograph in a Power-
Point presentation) is actually from the ending of his first fast. He did
three public fasts and did numerous more personal private fasts. For
him, fasting was a way of cleansing and becoming more in tune and
more connected with what he saw as his broader mission in fighting
for farm workers. It was very difficult and oftentimes hard to remove
oneself from the day-to-day struggles that the farm workers were facing, to look at what it meant to build a movement that would continue
to advocate and support them beyond just that one day. For him, many
times, fasting became an opportunity to almost visualize what the future
could hold for farm workers, but it was also a very personal sacrifice and
recommitment to his work.

In 1968 he participated in his first public fast, and it was his fast for
nonviolence. The reason why it was called that was because many of the

farm workers were becoming frustrated. They had been on strike from 1965 to 1963, so for three years, many of them faced and were literally hit with the brutal clubs of the local police and other kinds of hired thugs and goons the owners would bring in to try to diminish and basically crush their organizing efforts. These farm workers looked at my grandfather and asked, how can you expect us to stand with nonviolence in the face of violence? How can you expect us to continue to maintain that when we're being hit with continuous violence? My grandfather knew that, if the farm workers chose violence, they would be destroyed both physically as well as a movement, as an organization. He knew that those who opposed him had more money and more resources and, for lack of a better word, bigger guns, and they could easily crush a violent uprising of farm workers. The deeper sense of nonviolence was that their message would not be clear to the general public if it was shared through the use of violence. Their message of dignity and respect of humanity would get lost if they engaged in violence and that is what would be reported, whether on the news, or shared through word of mouth in the grass-roots effort. The result would be that this would become another one of those violent uprisings rather than a struggle for dignity and humanity and respect.

He fasted for twenty-five days; it was a water-only fast. He didn't know how the farm workers were going to react to it. In fact, some of them were puzzled. They were saying: "Here we are getting crushed in the strike and you're going to stop eating? How does that make sense? What's that going to do for our cause?" They not only didn't understand the concept of fasting, but when they witnessed the level of personal sacrifice he was willing to endure and engage in, not eating and growing weak, they asked themselves, if he's willing to do this much, then what am I willing to do? What is it I can do for the cause? Like most of his actions and efforts, it was never about dictating to others what they needed to do or what they should or should not do, it was him leading by example, showing and modeling what could be done, what was possible, and in terms of the heading of this talk, the concept of *Sí se puede* (Yes we can!).

He knew it wasn't enough to just tell them; he needed to show them that this was a road they had to walk down together, hand in hand, organizer and organizer. He never saw himself as a union leader and was frustrated by that label. For him, he was always an organizer. He said organizers have to work hard and never give up; that was how he saw himself and how he saw each and every farm worker and each and every supporter he worked with. There was a slogan for a while that was: "Every worker is an organizer." It is a concept that each one of us has that potential to change our conditions, our lives, and our situation.

Earlier, I was questioned about the way folks communicated during this time, and I can't help but smile, because here is the Western Union telegram (referring to a photograph in a PowerPoint presentation). Talk about dated communication. Obviously, this was before the age of e-mail, Facebook, and MySpace, and all those great social networking sites and Twitter and ways of getting information out and gathering information in. The telegram was sent to my grandfather by Dr. Martin Luther King Jr. — unfortunately the two never met before Dr. King was assassinated — but there was obviously a common solidarity each of them saw and articulated. It is eloquently articulated in Dr. King's telegram. This was during the 1968 fast as well, the fast for nonviolence. For me, what is so important about this telegram is the excerpt where he said, the plight of your people and ours is so grave, we all need the inspiring example and effective leadership you have given.

To talk about and think about that commonality and solidarity of people's fight for justice, fight for peace, fight for a better life, to me, this telegram was an important validation of my grandfather's work. You see, he was a student of Dr. King, and most people don't talk about this because we rarely talk about all the people who have influenced our great leaders. We only talk about our great leaders, right?

Dr. King influenced my grandfather, and you saw that in many of the tactics he chose to use. In 1968, right around this time, the farm workers engaged in the boycott of grapes; some of you may have participated in that boycott. The boycott was a direct result of seeing the successes of the Montgomery Bus Boycott and what that did for the Civil Rights Movement. It put the Civil Rights Movement on the national scene, to give folks anywhere an opportunity to stand up or sit down for civil rights. That's what the grape boycott did for the Farm Worker Movement. It didn't matter if you were a soccer mom in Kansas or a student in New York City or a factory worker out in Chicago, you could support farm workers by not buying grapes. You didn't have to live near a field or even pick up a picket sign, but through your own actions, you could do something to support farm workers.

The boycott was one example, but so were the marches up and down the valleys of California, and even out into Arizona. This next picture (referring to a photograph in a PowerPoint presentation) is of my grandfather and Coretta Scott King during his second public fast, which was his fast for love. The Arizona governor at that time wanted to make it illegal for farm workers to organize and associate in large groups. It is a law still on the books today. Farm workers do not have the right to organize in Arizona and are not covered by the National Labor Relations Act. I don't know how many of you know that, but farm workers and backstretch workers — backstretch workers work in the race track with horses and they take care of the grounds keeping and the horses — are the only two categories of workers left out of the National Labor Relations Act in the 1930s. This act passed with the support of Southern legislators who said they would sign the act, but don't touch our work force. It was a typical example of nimbyism ("Not In My Back Yard"). Arizona took it a step further and actually put laws on the books that farm workers couldn't organize. In 1975, California signed the Agriculture Labor Relations Act into law, allowing farm workers the right to organize, and it is the only state in the entire United States that did so, and to this day, it is still the only one on the books. This seems absurd in this day and age. I already mentioned the boycott but these are some lovely signs of the boycott from grapes.

Later, there was a lettuce boycott, and I think in 1975, a Gallup poll said about seventeen million Americans had boycotted lettuce or grapes. This is what I like to talk to young people about. Oftentimes when I share the story of my grandfather and his ability to effect change, despite the fact that he came from humble beginnings and did not have a lot of formal education, I tell them, here was this small brown man who impacted seventeen million people to take action. That's a pretty significant thing when you think about it. That was before people had access to information and networks and other ways to build support and enact change that exist today. I always joke around and say, had Facebook been around back in the day, maybe my grandfather and Dr. King would have been friends and sent each other notes and stuff.

For my grandfather, throughout his lifetime, service was more than just an action. It was more than just an act, and more than just something good to do on a Sunday afternoon; it was a way of life. He saw it as both a personal mandate and a social mandate. He saw it as part of being Catholic and part of being an American. This is the mandate he was given to ensure the concept of liberty and justice for all. He knew it wasn't liberty and justice for all, except for farm workers. That's what he wanted people to understand and realize. Whether it was his personal or social mandate that compelled his actions, it existed throughout his lifetime. He passed away at the age of sixty-six. He was young. His father lived to be 102. His mother lived to be ninety-nine. We all assumed he would live forever. When he passed away in 1993, it was shocking for all of us, but we began to realize that he had worked tirelessly throughout his life. He was able to condense 120 years of life into sixty-six years.

What I like to remind folks is not that we need to cram 120 years of life into sixty-six, but that we can live out that 120 years by accomplishing these acts of service and continuing to realize the potential each and every one of us has, not just for ourselves but for the betterment of our community and society. I think we're living in an important time in our history, in the history of not just this country but in the history of the world. To me it's exciting and hopeful, and not just because that was the campaign slogan. When we think about the lessons my grandfather instilled in each of us and his continued legacy, it's not just for keeping his name and face present, but for looking more critically and deeply at what he stood for and how he lived his life. Why was it that, unlike others who had tried for hundreds of years, he was able to succeed in organizing farm workers? It wasn't because he was special or because he had any wealth or resources at his disposal, but it was about his commitment and compassion for people, his compassion for the farm workers. He knew he couldn't live another day of his life without living it in service of the farm workers. I learned that at an early age; I grew up being able to participate in some of the marches and actions taking place around immigration; I was able to not just touch but be part of a legacy that continues until this day.

My grandfather said: "Once social change begins, it cannot be reversed. You cannot un-educate the person who has learned to read. You cannot humiliate the person who feels pride. You cannot oppress the people who are not afraid anymore."

I feel this quote captures that essence, not about a person, not about an individual, not about a man, and not about my grandfather, but about that deeper mission, the common cause we find in the real example for leadership and change he gave us. Not that he possessed it alone; we can find it sometimes in our parents, in our brothers and sisters, in our mentors, or maybe in those we choose to mentor, but we have that deep connection.

These are the lessons I learned throughout my lifetime. I had the fortune of attending UC Berkeley. I know I spoke ill of them before, but only because I have the authority to do so now that I am a Golden Bear. I appreciated my time at Berkeley; it was a wonderful place. I had the fortune of attending Berkeley and earning a degree in Latin American Studies. Through that experience I expanded my knowledge tremendously and was able to make connections between my experiences with the farm workers and my broader experiences throughout Latin America and the world.

One lesson I learned in college was to realize that the deepest, most profound experiences I had throughout my lifetime were my most important and lasting lessons. Growing up in the Farm Worker Movement was my classroom. In many ways it was my university, and bringing that experience into this institution was prestigious and important, and to me, a powerful opportunity. The experiences of growing up in the Farm Worker Movement and being with my grandfather — having him not just as a grandfather but a mentor — and growing up with my mother, father, and grandmother, all of them have been powerful examples and role models for me. I learned that we have only one life to live, and it's how we choose our purpose in life that determines who we are as people, as individuals. I learned what it means to sacrifice, to give my time and my energy and skills and talents to something I care about, regardless of what reward there might be in return, which is usually a deeper personal reward than anything material could ever be. I learned what it means to have courage; even getting up in front of you today is not an easy thing to do. I get nervous before all my speaking engagements. I am comforted by the words of my grandfather when he said, "When you stop getting nervous, it means you don't care." Having that courage and trusting others enough to give a part of myself to others is an important lesson I learned growing up in the Farm Worker Movement. I also learned what it means to give yourself to a cause that is bigger than you or any one person. That is the important lesson about my grandfather, it was never about him; it was never about anything but the farm workers themselves.

I want to share a quote that, to me, signifies who my grandfather was. He said, "It was never about grapes or lettuce, but always about people." I am going to be critical of activists right now, so please forgive me. Sometimes in our activism we get so caught up in the issues that we forget about the humanity, the common humanity even between individuals. Nothing pains me more than to go into an organization that is fighting for social justice and finding out that people are treating one another like enemies or treating one another competitively in this arena.

We have to start from within; we have to begin that transformation on a personal level but also within our organizations and institutions. I was reminded of this today while listening to President Obama speak from Ghana, where he visited the Cathedral where many slaves were held before they were shipped across the Atlantic. One of the things he said was that, while this is obviously a devastating part of our history, we all need to find that sense of personal responsibility and self-determination in the wounds that still exist. I think that this is an important message for us to discuss and bring forward today. Had my grandfather not assumed his responsibility as a former farm worker to advocate and fight for the rights of all farm workers, conditions today would be much worse.

That is true about many people, so we need to see what our personal responsibility is — maybe it's not based on our own experiences of oppression or injustice or struggle — and find that compassion and connection with others, that common connection of humanity and humanness. The fact is, we all want a better livelihood for ourselves, our families, and our communities, so why can't we come together and, as a people, understand that nothing is inherently corrupt. Even as it relates to my grandfather and to the Farm Worker Movement, he oftentimes said that not all farm workers were angels and not all growers were devils. Nothing inherent in any of our systems makes us either supporters or opponents, so how are we going to make those choices?

How are we going to carry out or build these institutions? How are we going to carry out our work? Too often we have a tendency to perpetuate the things we find most disturbing or want to change. Doesn't it begin with our own personal transformation, but not stopping there, how that transformation will impacts others? My grandfather talked about it in terms of an education of the heart, and that is a lot of the work I am involved in now. Actually, the name of the initiative I helped run for the Chávez Foundation is the "Educating the Heart" school program.

My grandfather said that education of the heart is not imparted by books, but by the loving touch of a teacher. For him, finding that compassion of shared humanity and connection is education of the heart. We talk about it a lot; our work is to create a connection between the head, the heart, and the hands for our students because that seems to be easily digestible for them. Your head, your academics, the knowledge and content and history connects with what you want to do with your life to effect change.

You need the compassion to move in the direction that betters yourself and others. You need your hands to put it into practice, because if we just live in our head and heart, nothing is going to change. We need to live out our values; we need to live out our beliefs, even if sometimes it is uncomfortable. We like to compartmentalize our lives so that our professional self is not always our personal self, or sometimes we can't be our whole self with our families or even some of our closest friends. Finding that opportunity and asking how to engage in living out our values is a way we can transform, not just our lives but our communities. That is what my grandfather did. It wasn't rocket science for him. It wasn't anything revolutionary per se. He would say, "Our revolution is winning because ours is a revolution of hearts and minds." It isn't a revolution about material or violent opposition, but about transforming how we think and interact, and how we engage and support one another, and by extension, our communities and our world.

As we gather here today to reflect on some of the lessons we have learned, I think it is important that we see the relevancy and the connection to us today. This isn't a historical time period that we can fold up and put on the shelf in a textbook, but one that continues to inform us today and can continue to evolve in our own work and actions.

I have mentioned to you some lessons I learned from my mother, and that's a photo (referring to a photograph in a PowerPoint presentation) of her and my grandfather. She unfortunately passed away in October 2000. Although she is not with us physically, she continues to support my growth and development and the other spiritual realm. When she passed away, my uncle also jokingly said: "I always knew she was Dad's favorite. He had to take her first." You can see the connection between the two here.

Here are also some lovely photos (referring to photographs in a PowerPoint presentation) of me as a child. I am to the right of my grandfather in a little white dress. If you look close, you can see I still look about the same; I am only a couple of inches taller, but that is when I was eight years old. That is the two of us in New York City; I think it was during the Labor Day Parade. Earlier we talked about communicating a message to the masses without some of the new technologies. Being present at Labor Day parades was a way of sharing your message through public action, and this public action became a huge component that the UFW did for years, even if it was in the form of human billboards. Some guerilla marketing tactics that are now infiltrating mainstream marketing are similar to some of those early organizing tactics we used. Now they have sign boards and people flipping them. We called that a human billboard, but we would take up three or four blocks and have supporters with big old signs talking about boycotting grapes and other issues that the farm workers were facing.

This photo (referring to a photograph in a PowerPoint presentation) is my first public speaking engagement. We were in New Jersey at a striking airline workers picket line. It was in the 1980s when the airline workers went on strike. There are those of you who might recall the wonderful Reagan era; Reagan decided he was going to fire all of them to demonstrate that organized labor had no real power in our country. I think it has had a significant impact on organized labor since then. We were supporting the airline workers. I thought we were going to just say hello to the workers and raise our fists in solidarity. Little did I know I was going to get a bullhorn shoved in my mouth at the age of ten to speak to and somehow inspire a group of workers.

The story I was asked to share that day was a story that had just happened to me and my sister. I was nine and my sister was twelve, and we were passing out leaflets in front of a supermarket, informing people about the use of pesticides sprayed on grapes. My sister, my father, and I were all arrested for violating private property rights. We knew we weren't violating private property rights, and had we been, we wouldn't have been out there handing out leaflets. But we were arrested. That was the first time I was arrested for political activism, but it wasn't the last time. I have been arrested a couple of times since and those are like my Brownie patches. All of it has been in line with my beliefs and values. I have had a couple of students ask me what that was like, and would I do it again. I shared with them that sometimes the consequences for our actions aren't always what we like or that we will be comfortable with, but if we are firm in our beliefs and actions, and if we are also nonviolent in our approach, we have the justness of our cause to carry us through. That's the message a lot of young people connect with and it resonates with them as they explore their own sense of activism and question authority in that way.

This is a more recent photo (referring to a photograph in a Power-Point presentation) of my father and me. My father is the current president of the United Farm Workers. He has continued in the tradition of my grandfather in ensuring that farm workers are treated with dignity and respect and seen as human beings and not as just part of a production cycle.

Here is a quote about the education of the heart:

> You should know that education of the heart is very important. This will distinguish you from others. Educating oneself is easy, but educating ourselves to help other human beings to help the community is much more difficult.

That is what I see as my work today, working with young people and engaging them. This concept of education of the heart is not just in words and not just in theory, but most important, through their own actions and service to their community. I found service to be a very transforming experience, in particular for young people who are in the process of exploring themselves, their relationships with one another, and their relationship with the world. It is a strong foundation that I know I was given as a young child, and I think all of our young people deserve, and that's the opportunity to experience our own gifts and talents, our own ability to make a change, however small that change might seem.

I will close with saying that we are in a time, although historic, that is also difficult. We haven't experienced economic times like we now find ourselves in, at least most of us, in our lifetime. I would hope it is a time we don't have to experience again, but I think what this time calls for is the type of commitment and service my grandfather instilled in me and many others who decided to stand up and fight for their rights and transform their condition. In this time of economic hardship, I think it is important that we ask ourselves what is it that we can do to be of service to others. I think, in doing so, we will find a whole new life full of meaning and full of love. That was what my grandfather and I experienced and continue to experience, and something I think all of us deserve the opportunity to experience.

My grandfather showed me that together, *Si se puede* (Yes we can!). I think that is an important message we need to share with others.

Thank you all.

July 11, 2009
SGI-USA Santa Monica Culture of Peace Resource Center

Gender Equality Is Essential to Achieving Development and to Building Just Societies

Yassine Fall

Senior Economic Advisor for the United Nations Development
Fund for Women (UNIFEM); President, African Women
Millennium Initiative on Poverty and Human Rights

Yassine Fall is the senior economic advisor for the United Nations Development Fund
for Women (UNIFEM) with twenty-seven years of field, policy, and management
experience. She is a founding member of several international networks including
the African Women Millennium Initiative on Poverty and Human Rights (AWOMI),
the Gender and Economic Reforms in Africa (GERA), the International Gender and
Trade Network (IGTN), and the Beijing Caucus for Economic Justice, which led to the
"Women's Eyes on the World Bank Campaign."

Before joining the United Nations, for twelve years she managed her own consul-
tancy firm (Economists for Social Transformation in Africa) working throughout the
continent, from economically challenged countries, urban slums, and rural areas to
countries in conflict and refugee camps, on assignment for various development agencies, focusing on issues ranging from macroeconomics and poverty analysis, international trade assessment, emergency relief operations, HIV/AIDS assessment, natural
resources management, land tenure, child labor studies, gender and development,
and food security.

Every two years, back in her country of Senegal, she organizes the Young Women
Knowledge and Leadership Institute (YOWLI), which brings about one hundred
young women and men from all regions of Africa and its Diaspora to learn, network,
and strategize for organized action to influence macroeconomics and international
policies.

Ms. Fall studied economics in Senegal, France, and the United States. She taught
mathematics and applied economics for five years in U.S. schools.

Yassine Fall touches on many of the eight action areas
defined in the 1999 United Nations Declaration and
Programme of Action on a Culture of Peace, most notably

the second, promoting sustainable economic and social development, and the fourth, ensuring equality between women and men.

She states: "You have to develop an economic model and policies by working backward from the bottom, working with people and empowering them. You need economic policies that start from people's needs like education, health, water, energy, and food. About food — you cannot develop a country without supporting the production of a food system. You cannot develop a country without supporting people to be healthy because a healthy human being is a democratic human being. A healthy human being is a productive being, a person who can stand up and work."

She also says, "My crusade is about revisiting economics from the point of view of the human being, from the point of view of human well-being instead of the point of view of market well-being."

It's a pleasure to be here. This is the kind of space I like to be in. I work for the United Nations, but I always like to engage with people who promote a sense of solidarity and humanity. I am from Senegal, Africa. I grew up in the suburbs of Dakar, in Pikine, with a father who was an Imam and a mother who was working. My father was also a farmer. I attended public schools, never private schools, and landed in the United States in New York in 1980 with my husband to go to Howard University in Washington, D.C. I did my graduate studies in economics. I went home in 1990 and came back in 2000 to work for the United Nations.

I have friends all around the world. I meet people from all walks of life, people who live in difficult situations, people who lack a voice. I also meet people who are decision makers. I work with women and young people in communities in Africa.

And all of them teach me. My experience is informed by the people I meet in my work and in my volunteer service. First, I learned that when you meet people, you need to listen. Listening is important for learning, and listening is something that is lacking today from leaders who make decisions that influence people's lives. As leaders learn to listen, they will be able to change this world. When leaders listen to the majority of the people, they will respond with policies that will produce better effects. If leaders listen, they will respect women more because they will see that women carry, in most parts of the world, the position of the well-being of people.

I was born in a village and I spent all my young life going back to the village every summer with my mother. I spent my vacations there and went to the fields to be with people who were suffering from famine and to work with children in schools. I have taken classes with teachers and realized that we all aspire to live a good decent life where there are services that people can enjoy, meaning access to good roads, clean water, public education, and health services that every human being in this world would like to have, but not every human being has. Many people in the world do not enjoy the basic social goods and services that human beings require. In my life of fifty-six years, I have seen that enjoyment of well-being, that enjoyment of social goods, if I may use that term, are diminishing for many people in the world.

My fight, my struggle, in my work or in my time as a volunteer worker, is always to use that time to contribute to improving equality and social justice, making sure that people who have no voice can be heard, and making sure that I can contribute to defining policies that improve the lives of people. That is my passion. It is my passion because I have seen rural areas that produce their foods and work hard to export that food daily in urban centers and I've seen many of those urban areas get poorer because particular programs didn't respond to the reality on the ground. I would like to work toward changing that, in other words, to reverse that trend. That is what keeps me going. What keeps me going is a sense of unfinished business, a sense of saying to myself, how do I want to be remembered? I don't want to be remembered as an economist from the United Nations. I want to be remembered as a person who touched the life of another person and helped that person improve his or her life.

I am happy to be here today because I was asked to talk about myself in a way that other people could relate to me. Where I grew up in Pikine was not seen as a well-to-do community, but we had many basic needs that people ask for today. We had access to education; we had access to healthcare. We had malaria, but today you can get treatment. If you go to school, you don't have to pay; it is free. You can have good teachers like anywhere else. I went to an elementary and high school. I was twelve years old when I first took transportation by myself to go to high school. My high school was John F. Kennedy High School, a girl's school and a school of excellence, where girls came from all parts of the country to study. So I went to high school and then I went to university. Until I went to university, I only went to all girls' schools. I went to boarding school in my senior year of high school.

In 1980 when the program suffered budget cuts, all of the boarding schools in my country, including the girls' boarding schools in my country, were closed. That was extremely unfortunate. I enjoyed going to boarding school. They were very good centers of learning that girls had access to. If you go to boarding school, you all wear the same uniform. You all eat the same food. Nobody knows whose father is a minister or whose father is a farmer, whose mother is a professor or whose mother is a stay-at-home mom. Everyone is treated the same way. The only difference is who studies well and does well and who advances. To me, this was a fantastic situation that taught me, while I was away from my family, to learn how to connect to people and learn how to share with other people who came from different regions of my country. That was the first economic shock of closing boarding schools.

The second thing I learned was when I went back to my village and saw a big corporation being opened. The corporation was allowed to take the land from the farmers, privatize the land, and start milling sugar to export. I saw, little by little, my cousins and uncles leaving the farm to work for the factory. Little by little, I saw them go on strike because the working conditions were so difficult, but they had already lost their land. I saw farmers not being able to produce rice and millet and beans because their land had been taken by the factory. I also saw a process of people being disempowered; I saw women working in filth, not going to work where the rice was produced; and I saw less and less food being produced locally.

The price of food was going up, and when I went back to my country, my cousins said, "Look at my hands, I have been pounding so much rice." I asked myself, why. Why was it that … I am advancing, but they were going backward? I was in boarding school and university and I came back to my community where I saw so many children out of school. When I was growing up everybody was in school. People would say to me, "You know, Muslim people don't go to school." My father was an Imam. But my mother said, "These girls are going to school." I remember the day my mother put me into school, and we stood in line. My mother convinced my father. We went in line but the line was closed. My mother came back to my dad and said, "You are the Imam, you have to write a letter." Finally my father wrote a letter and I was accepted in the school.

The first time I went to school was the first time I saw a white person, the director of my school. I went back to my mother and tried to explain what her hair looked like. My father always told us, you go to school, you study. If you do not study, you come back and go into the kitchen. We knew, my sister and I, that there was no after-school class. You had no choice. You had to study, because you knew if you didn't study, what you would come back to. So it was an empowering process to go to school and come home. My mom didn't know how to read or write, and I taught her what I learned every day. She told me, I can look and see that you aren't studying your lesson! Study now. It was such a very empowering process to follow until after high school, until university, just to be considered on the basis of my merits. I could do well and move on.

When I finished high school, I had a choice between teaching and going to university. My father told me to go to university. I said, no, I want to teach so I can make money and bring lights and cold water into our house. My father said no, we have been living like this all our lives. You go on. You have a mission.

So I continued my studies. I wanted to be an economist, because I kept saying to myself, I don't understand what programs are being developed. In the past, you could come back to the village after the harvest and see all kinds of food on the train and be very proud and happy of your street because the harvest resulted in neighbors receiving cocoa and millet. Now when you go out to the village, people are suffering. What happened? What is going on? What kind of program is this? That was my first curiosity. I was told economists were behind the minister of finance and were developing the policies and implementing them. These were the people that had the knowledge. I said to myself that I need to have this knowledge also so I can understand what they are doing that is wrong and help to change that.

When I finished high school, I was asked to study Spanish, so I took three years of Spanish at university. I saved my money and traveled to France, because I wanted to study economics. The system in school wouldn't allow me to study economics because I had to go teach Spanish. So I went to France and all my friends were saying, "Yassine, doing economics is very hard because you need to know a lot of mathematics." I said, "Is it just something you study?" They said yes and I said, "I can do it."

I laughed at the boy who said that I could not do it. But I said that as long as I have a brain and can study, I can do it. I went to the library. There is a library close to Sorbonne University. I used to take math books to that library every day and study my math and my economics until I finished my first degree. My husband was a journalist, and he was teaching at that time at the university until he finished his masters. He was leading a group of journalists who were trying to bring freedom of the press and independent newspapers to all of Africa. He was told that if he continued this, he was going to be fired from the university. He ultimately got fired. He called me one day from Senegal — I was in France finishing my studies before going home. He told me that he called me because he wanted to study telecommunications.

I said: "What? I'm going back home." He said no. He said he wanted to study new communication technology because it was the future — telecommunications and information science. So he came to France and worked for a year as a news journalist, saving money. Then, he said he wanted to go to America. I said again: "What? No! I don't want to go to America." This was in 1979. He said that I could study at Howard University, but I said that I was scared to go to America; that I had not heard good things about America.

My husband said that if I went to America, I could study English and go to graduate school, etc. Finally he convinced me, and I came to America. We studied English for three months. He went to Harvard

University to get his PhD, and I came with my son who was ten months old. I continued my studies and was also teaching at the language lab at Howard University. That's when I started my dream in America. It was an interesting journey. I made so many friends and met so many people at the university. I experienced wonderful times of learning and exchange in America.

That's why I continued my studies in economics and got to know groups of women from Africa in Washington, D.C. I went home every summer. I worked for community groups and women's groups and family courts at home. There was a big debate in my country at that time about women's rights and family court and the relationship between the man and the family. When I finished my studies at Howard University, my husband and I went home to work. He was working for a university, and I started out as a consultant and then started traveling. My interest was to see how I could translate the economic development I had learned and apply it to the community level. I did not want to work in a bank or in the ministry. I wanted to see what people were doing.

I was shocked to see the role women were playing in these communities, families, and households. I started writing about it after interviewing women and explaining finance to them. While participating in discussions with these women, I told them that their version of economics was wrong because it interfered with their reality. You need to observe the situations of people. You need to look at what people are doing, what people are saying, what they are selling. You need to see what the needs of the people are and then you need to find out what the problems are that the people are facing.

From the problems that people are facing, you can simply develop an economic model. The economic model is a simplification of the reality of the people. That simplification is the basis for what we are calculating as growth rates. But if that model doesn't represent a reality that can produce change, then it is not a good model. You have a bad economic model because what you are developing are policies that are ill-conceived because they are not based on reality, they are not based on people's needs or on what people can do to develop themselves.

You have to develop an economic model and policies by working backward from the bottom, working with people and empowering them

You need economic policies that start from people's needs like education, health, water, energy, and food. About food — you cannot develop a country without supporting the production of a food system. You cannot develop a country without supporting people to be healthy because a healthy human being is a democratic human being. A healthy human being is a productive human being, a person who can stand up and work. You need to develop economies of people who are educated and informed.

My crusade is about revisiting economics from the point of view of the human being, from the point of view of human well-being instead of the point of view of market well-being.

In Africa, we have had our share of economic and financial crises. Actually, every time there is a crisis in the developed world, the solution is to solve the crisis by pushing it upon a poor country or poor person. We had been told since 1980 to leave our markets loose, open our markets, be nice to investors and let them come, fire and hire at peace. Let them destroy the environment. Be open for full investment. Let the companies come and make money, then close down the thing and leave. As long as the market is good, it is good. No! Because corporate power can make profits, it doesn't mean my life is better, it doesn't mean I'm informed, it doesn't mean I'm progressing.

Economics should be reversed. That's my crusade, to challenge economics as it is being done today; to challenge it from my knowledge and challenge it from my life experience. My life experience is informed by the people I meet, people I listen to, people I interview who present their life with an economic language an economist can understand. I can sit face to face with any economist and I'm not afraid because I know I talk sense. I know I say something that resonates in the lives of people, but it must be something that improves the lives of human beings.

I was happy when I met young people and they challenged me and asked questions, because the questions they were asking were already the kind of questions I was asking myself in terms of ensuring that they would have a more equal world or have a more just world. When we are all contributing to increasing the fruits of society, how can we have better distributing mechanisms that ensure that we all benefit; that the corporations do not benefit, do not lend money, make money, reinvest it, while we continue to pay. How can we reverse that? That is the fundamental question of humanity in a just world.

I was saying earlier that in order to have a just world, it is not about peace only. It is about first promoting equality and social justice. Promoting social justice by diminishing the number of people who feel hungry, who feel utterly uneducated, who are not healthy, who have nothing to lose. Let us not kill one another. When you have more people who have nothing to lose, you have ranks of people who can be brought into violence.

My life has been inspired by many people — my parents, my grandparents, my children, and my friends.

Working at the United Nations, I often find myself in awkward situations because I have to be a diplomat and I'm not a good diplomat. The United Nations is an association of member states, and it is also an association of states where the powerful have a big voice. Recently, we had a summit on global finance and economic crises with well-known economists attending, like Joseph Stiglitz and like Jomo Kwame Sundaram, who has served as the United Nations Assistant Secretary-General for Economic Development in the United Nations Department of Economic and Social Affairs (DESA) since 2005. He is a great economist from Malaysia, whose father named him after two great Africans: Kwame Nkrumah and Jomo Kenyatta. This group of thinkers from all around the world may produce a report that resonates with what we say. If so, they will present it to the United Nations Assembly, where every year the members take a vote. One country designates a person to be the president of the Assembly; now the president is from Nicaragua.

It was a very heated discussion. The developed countries were saying that the economic system we have is good. We just have to bring stimulus packages and re-energize the market, and the market will produce and trickle down to people and the people will be better. Many people in Nicaragua and other places were saying that we needed to change the development paradigm. We needed to change the economic system to be a better and more just system where developing people, where poor people who have less, where elderly, where younger people, where women have a better voice, have a better share. This was a big debate. It was a debate that we see also in other countries because of corporations. They want to keep the status quo. They say: "Just give me more money. I am going to fix my company that is falling apart, and then life will be better." I don't know about that. Compare that to people who say, "Let us go to those people who are losing their houses, those people who have no access. Let us see how we can re-energize them, because there are many ways of energizing economics." I learned that, for the past twenty years, we have been using one way, which is market driven, supply as force economics. The corporations are producing for supply. Let us do demand-driven. Let us try to connect workers and put money and employment in their pockets. Let's try to make more demand for human services than for economics. That is what was done after the Great Depression and the New Deal. That was killed when I came here in the 1980s and that was the '80s way to say, "That's the market." I remember when I saw President Ronald Reagan on TV; he was talking about the fundamentals of the market. The market is strong; let's promote private companies. Now we see corporations acting really wild. We see pharmaceutical companies acting extremely wild. You cannot leave the lives of people to the private sector only. The market's goal is to make profits — minimize cost, maximize profits. You go to China and employ people at low cost, you make a profit; you go Thailand, you go to Fiji, you go to Vietnam. You minimize cost and maximize profits. That's what the market does. Let the market do that, but we cannot take that to be the mantra for everything.

You cannot take the market and use it to provide things people need — the states have to provide social goods. That is what is happening today in the world. We need citizens who are enlightened crusaders in front, because I believe in the power of numbers. I believe in the power of solidarity. I believe in the power of many people saying, "This is the way it should be done," and it happens. We need that in the world. We need people who are saying that we need to promote humanity. Humanity means that we ensure that every human being in this world is like me. What I want for me, what I want for my children, I want for you. I want for your children too. That is possible; that is doable.

The world has never been as wealthy as it is today, but there is so much inequality, inequality is increasing. When I watch TV, I see people who have worked all their lives lose their homes because of banks, and I get heartbroken. Banks cannot be left alone. They need to be regulated. They need to be watched very closely like milk on the fat, because the banks are enterprises for making money. They sell money to make a profit. That is the job of a bank. You can say it in a much more sophisticated way through housing or insurance, but the role of a bank is an enterprise that sells money to make a profit. Now, you cannot let an enterprise that is only interested in showing shareholders how much money they have made be left alone without being watched very closely.

I get inspired by people, people like you who share the same vision and hope like me, but who have your own role. I have my own role. My role is, I study economics and I think things out. Everywhere I go, I want to meet with economists and policy makers to spread the message of a correct economics, an economics that centers on human beings.

Thank you very much for having me.

August 13, 2009
SGI-USA New York Culture of Peace Resource Center

Climate Change and the Sustainability of Mankind

Overcoming the Inner Limits

Ervin Laszlo

President and Co-founder, The Club of Budapest; Co-chair, World Wisdom Council, author of eighty-five books; and twice nominated for the Nobel Peace Prize

Ervin Laszlo is a Hungarian philosopher of science, systems theorist, integral theorist, and originally a classical pianist.

Dr. Laszlo is generally recognized as the founder of systems philosophy and general evolution theory. His work in recent years has centered on the formulation and development of the "Akasha Paradigm," the new conception of cosmos, life, and consciousness emerging at the forefront of the contemporary sciences. He serves as president of The Club of Budapest, chairman of the Ervin Laszlo Center for Advanced Study, chancellor of the Giordano Bruno New-Paradigm University, and editor of *World Futures: The Journal of New Paradigm Research*.

He is recipient of the highest degree in philosophy and human sciences from the Sorbonne, the University of Paris, as well as of the coveted Artist Diploma of the Liszt Ferenc Academy of Budapest. Additional prizes and awards include four honorary doctorates.

For many years, he has served as president of The Club of Budapest, which he founded. He is an advisor to the UNESCO director general, ambassador of the International Delphic Council, member of the International Academy of Science, World Academy of Arts and Science, and the International Academy of Philosophy.

Twice nominated for the Nobel Peace Prize (2004, 2005), he received the Goi Peace Prize (2001). He has authored more than eighty books, which have been translated into twenty languages, and has published in excess of four hundred articles and research papers, including six volumes of piano recordings.

Ervin Laszlo addresses several of the eight action areas defined in the 1999 United Nations Declaration and Programme of Action on a Culture of Peace, particularly the second, promoting sustainable economic and social development.

Dr. Laszlo states, "What we are doing is creating a consciousness that can bring about peace and sustainability with the values of a global community that can live in harmony with nature."

He further states: "A new world peace is being born before our eyes. It is being born by a small group of people creating a new mindset among themselves, and it is being born. This group will find a way to reach one another and play a catalytic role, a role of helping people join together to become a force, a force that is sufficient to launch a change for the world."

My message is particularly apt and relevant to people entering a spiritual path. Our task is nothing less than to create a new civilization. The civilization currently dominant in the world has had its day. We have reached a transition point and it's up to us to facilitate it. There is a lot of media hype that it is the end of the world, but instead, it is a transition to a different world, a natural outgrowth of this one, which is coming and it is a natural development. It is not artificial. We are not going to genetically modify the human species. What we are doing is creating a consciousness that can bring about peace and sustainability with the values of a global community that can live in harmony with nature.

We are a planetary species and we have to live as a planetary civilization. It is easier said than done, but it is being done and it is not utopian. A new world peace is being born before our eyes. It is being born by a small group of people creating a new mindset among themselves, and it is being born. This group will find a way to reach one another and play a catalytic role, a role of helping people join together to become a force, a force that is sufficient to launch a change for the world.

Now the great anthropologist, Margaret Mead, has said, "Never doubt that a small group of thoughtful, committed citizens can change the world; indeed, it's the only thing that ever has." She added that nothing else ever has. But certainly, as we approach the end of an era, change becomes necessary. Committed people are the architects of the new order of the new world.

I would like to review the essential elements of this shift that we call the global shift. The key element is a change of consciousness, which means a change in values, a change in beliefs, and a change in ethics. It is not an artificial change; it's a natural change; it's a development; it's a growth. It's a growth, not in power, but in constructive power, not in power as it was. It's a growth in our ability to conceive of ourselves and our world, as belonging together and making one family.

I will get to the practical issues in a moment, but I want to begin with conceptual issues. We are all complex systems. We are systems simply because we consist of interactive parts that are so coherent, so well tuned that they can act as one. Thousands of chemical reactions occur every second in our bodies. All of that is coherent. All of that is tuned to a single overriding objective: to stay alive so that we can develop and contribute to the perfect growth of ourselves. The different cultures and societies also have to be coherent and oriented to our growth. As they do so, they will have an opportunity to redeem themselves.

The resources on the surface of our planet, however, need to be used sustainably and well. In the past, societies used them sustainably. In nearly the entire twenty thousand- or thirty thousand-year history of humanity, people used their resources sustainably because each environment had what you would now call "carrying capacity." This carrying capacity was the limit within which societies could operate. By the end of the last century (the twentieth), humanity had reached a global level; it had populated the entire planet. It was at this point that humanity began to overuse the carrying capacity of this planet. No matter what we look at or what measures we take, whether it is the carbon footprint, the ecological footprint, or the amount of water we use, we have certain constraints in what we can use sustainably without destroying our environment. This is the story of our future.

We are now, according to some calculations, using two and a half times the ecological resources of the planet. That means we need another planet and a half to supply us with these resources to remain on a sustainable basis. So we are facing a choice. One choice is we can dominate the world, to use these resources to serve our immediate selfish purposes and suffer the consequences. This kind of thinking is manipulative thinking. It has developed because a small percentage of the global civilization dominates the rest and is looking out only for its own interest; as such, it is like a cancer that grows on its own power for its own sake and eventually destroys its host.

Let's look at the way this world can change. Change is a very important factor. We are on the threshold of the winds of change. A year ago [2008], Barack Obama was elected president of the United States on the idea that we must change, and that, yes, we can change. Many are wondering if those changes can be really effective and how much of that change can be effective, but we do know that change has to happen, so we had better find out something about the dynamics of change.

Here is what I want to show you. First of all, in reviewing our situation, I won't spend much time on the scientific basis, but just illustrate why change is so necessary. The first thing to keep in mind is that we live on a planet. Here what you see as a planet is a large circle (referring to a photograph in a PowerPoint presentation). This is the surface of the earth. The surface of the earth is bathed in sunlight, in sunshine. This is what gives life to the earth. Everything that happens on the earth is driven by solar energy, either directly or indirectly. Even fossil energy is energy from the sun that has been stored on the earth for hundreds of thousands of years.

The immediate solarization is the basis. It is transformed by plants into biomass for photosynthesis. One plant is the food for another and food for animals. There is a whole food chain that uses the energy, transforms it, cycles it, and recycles it. Even when animals and plants die, they go back into the soil and fertilize the soil and they give energy for others. The point I want to make is a very simple one. Nature is an efficient, perfectly sustainable system that has existed for four billion years (about 600 million years for certain species), and operates as a highly efficient organism. It has been called the Gaia theory for the earth, almost like a living organism; it maintains itself, and further, it is efficient and sustainable.

Now what happened? About ten thousand years ago came another system and that was a human system. Communities of humans in the Middle East learned the art of domesticating plants. Domesticating plants means that they used the big rivers such as the Nile to irrigate the soil. They used the seeds that they found, planted them, used irrigation, and developed a food supply.

From that point onward, you see, humanity didn't just fit itself into the environment, it created an environment in which to fit itself, but it was still OK. Even though it polluted here and there — for example, it used up too much of the forest in the Middle East — but it still maintained itself. This kind of community, the Neolithic Revolution spread into Asia, Europe, and Africa.

This eventually resulted in a major shift in the modern age in the Western world, a critical shift that will always be looked upon in history books and in the public mind as a tremendous improvement and sign of progress. It may have been progress in certain respects, certainly in terms of technology and convenience, but it also brought about a great danger, because this shift was based on a mistaken notion of the world.

This notion is that the world around us is infinite in all relevant respects. In other words, all the resources we need whether water or minerals or biological substances are available in an infinite supply. Whatever we need, the earth can supply, and whatever we don't want and don't need will be used up because it will go back into the earth and the earth is an infinite sink. Of course, this appeared like five thousand years ago. It appeared like this in the Middle Ages, but when humanity reached one billion people on the planet in 1850, it started growing exponentially, developed technologies like burning coal and oil, and moved into the nuclear era. The use of these enormous powers transformed more and more of the resources of the earth to satisfy humanity's needs and interests. Of course, this notion of the earth having an infinite supply of resources turned out to be a fallacy. It turned out to be a mistake. Human beings created a second system and superimposed it on nature's system. The natural system is there, but we have created a system that operates in our own interests. Nature operates on genetic information, and genetic information can be changed, but it changes slowly. It takes thousands of years for mutations to change clearly in a species. It can take five thousand to fifty thousand years and much longer.

The way our human systems operate is by cultural information, by information of knowledge, information in the form of values, and information in the form of beliefs. We are now in a different information phase — the Internet, the way we talk to one another, our newspapers, our schools — everything around us are depositories of this kind of cultural information.

The kind of information on which this human system is now based makes for nonsustainability. It makes for the overuse of nature's system. We have overused it for about one hundred or one hundred fifty years. Now it has become greed. Even in my childhood, when a teacher asked a child to draw a sign of progress, many would draw a smoking smokestack. Industry was a sign of progress then and produced what we wanted. That the smoke could be toxic, that you couldn't breathe it; we didn't realize at the time how toxic it could be. Would it simply go away? The thinking was, all we had to do was build a high enough smokestack, and the smoke would disappear into the air. We thought you could throw things into the river, the river would take it down to the sea, and in the sea it would be safe and not impact the water supply.

Who could have imagined more than fifty years ago that we could pollute the planet's entire atmosphere? Who could have imagined that we could pollute the seas by throwing plastic bottles into them? Now they interfere with production of marine life in the Pacific and Indian Oceans and some parts of the Atlantic Ocean as well. We are living on a planet. We didn't take that seriously. Now we know that everything we do to the planet doesn't go away; it all comes back and affects public life. It's a very different mentality. I want you to understand that, because the change that will be required will not depend uniquely on money. Certainly it will not depend on power, and especially military power, which I think is useless. The real power will be the change in our consciousness.

I want to explain why I believe that the kind of worldview you are developing and that you have to worry about now is based on the Buddhist world view, which is so very relevant today. We come now to the promotion of progress in the world.

We used to think of progress as linear. Linear means that every time we do something we can add to it and make it a little better. If we add a little more for some things, that will improve the other things, bit by bit, year by year, more gross domestic product (GDP), more highway miles, more population, more education, all of this bit by bit. These were the beliefs throughout the nineteenth century and most of the twentieth century.

Throughout the second half of the twentieth century, it turned out that progress is circular, not linear, because progress takes place in the development of what I mentioned earlier, complex systems. It takes place in systems that have to maintain themselves in their environment by constantly taking in energy, information, material matter, and constantly using it for our daily lives. For that we have to be highly selective and highly coherent. This kind of system is never entirely stable and has all these fluctuations. *Fluctuation* is a word used in thermodynamics to show that the system is never exactly the same. It changes constantly.

For example, think of yourself as such a system. If you measure any of the parameters of your body, such as your heartbeat, the sugar in your blood, and the temperature of your body, you will find that they can vary. However, the body has what is known as a homeostatic mechanism, a homeostatic system that maintains internal equilibrium. As long as we are healthy, we constantly maintain our temperature, and all of the other vital parameters of our body.

We can say the same thing about society. As a society, if it is healthy and able to maintain itself, these parameters are kept in balance. Just like criminality is kept within bounds and asocial behavior is kept within bounds, the use of the environment should be kept within bounds. A healthy society is a sustainable society. Of course, if this is done peacefully, by using the voluntary commitment of people, it is far better than if it is by dictatorial measures that keep it in balance.

There is a point reached in the life and existence of every complex situation, however, where the fluctuations become so violent and great that they can no longer be pulled back. At that point, what happens to the individual: the individual dies. What happens to the species? The species reproduces and continues. A society doesn't have to die, meaning, become extinct. A society can change because a society, as I mentioned, is not based on genetic information that we cannot change. It is based on cultural information that we can change.

As societies changed over the centuries, over the millennium, they reached the limits of sustainability in a given environment. Then they adopted transvalue systems, different views, different needs, and a different kind of consciousness. The belief that we so often hear about the typical consciousness of the Western world is that human nature means to be greedy, seek power, and always want to out-compete everybody just to be the fittest and never mind others. This is not human nature. For millennia, human nature has meant being a social being, a member of a community in the embrace of nature. Traditional people have this sustainability. Traditional people don't break down. Typically the great Eastern traditions have been sustained and still operate sustainably.

Human nature is to be part of the world, otherwise we wouldn't be here. We wouldn't have lasted five million years. We have lasted thirty thousand years since we developed a culture that we call Homo sapiens. When we have the introduction of fluctuations, we can change, and we must change, because at that point we either break down and collapse or we can break through. If we break down, the recipe for change is very simple, go and change!

If you want to remain viable, if you want to sustain yourself and your society, you have to change. First you find a new attitude. A new attitude means a new harmony, a new coherence. The old kind of coherence is breaking down; it is taking us toward a collapse. We need to figure out what we want.

I will show you just one thing and afterward, I can talk about this more if you like. To find a new dynamic balance, we can benefit from our intuitive oneness with the world around us, an intuitive oneness I have researched on the basis of quantum physics, quantum biology, and quantum brain research, that is, the unified field that is the basis of all things. This is a connector (referring to a photograph in a PowerPoint presentation), a connection between things you enter into in meditation. Traditional people have always used it in their societies. When we pick up this sense of oneness and sense of belonging to others, we can feel others around us; we can feel nature around us. In a typical modern mentality, we have suppressed this.

This basic oneness or field is called the Akashic field in my work, and for simple reference I call it the A field. The A field is now beginning to be accepted in society and in science as being just as fundamental, if not more fundamental, than the electromagnetic and gravitational field. A field is the origin of all things. It is the *aether*. More than five thousand years ago the Akasha was known in India. It was known as the most fundamental dimension of all things.

Fortunately, there is a new rise in spirituality. There is a new rise in the search for understanding and a new rise in the experience of intuition of insight. A new mentality is arising, and it is coming about because people are seeking to understand themselves in the new world. Our brain is a highly sophisticated instrument. There is much more to it than we are using in the Western materialist-productionist context. We not only have our eyes and ears and a total of five sensory organs to understand or receive information from the world; nowadays our brain is being recognized, in new brain research circles, as a microscopic quantum system. I say microscopic because quantum systems have been known to exist on the super microscopic scale among quanta.

Since the 1980s it has been recognized that all quanta in the world are connected instantly with one another, some much more than others. Quanta have been in the same state. They can separate and remain connected. We know that the entire realm of atoms can be connected with one another. They may even have quantum computers in the future, which would be used in this kind of instant quanta connection. They would be connected by the instant transmission of information.

Before the 1980s and 1990s, it was known that super microscopic quanta are instantly connected. In the last ten or fifteen years, it has increasingly become known that the living world is connected in this way. What happens to one part of the living world happens also to others. The information is transferred because our brain is a super quantum computer in the sense that it can pick up information going way beyond the scope of sensitivity. It can pick up information from any part of the world. We notice this in altered states. In altered states, the brain opens its capacity, it no longer represses it, and allows this information to come into full consciousness.

Practicing meditation and believing is, in fact, knowing that the world consists of more than just matter and energy and space. It consists also of a deep layer of information that is the source of creativity, the source of evolution that makes for development. It is never individual development. It is always a co-development, a co-evolution, a co-origination, as we said, in individual stages.

We are in a situation where, if we can open up to this, we can find the next level of this dynamic balance, the harmony whereby we can live peacefully and justly. My great hope is that the consciousness evolution is the key to finding a new civilization facilitated by people who turn to their own consciousness and evolve by allowing their consciousness to reflect their unity. Then they will espouse new values, the kind of values and behaviors that will enable seven billion people in this world to live peacefully, justly, and sustainably.

This is the importance of the new rise of spirituality as it meets the new sciences. The intuitions that come into your mind in meditation are information from the world that needs to be put to good use because they inform you. The word *information* is being used in this context in the way the great physicist David Bohm used it, which is with a hyphen, "in-formation." It is not pure energy, the kind of energy that pushes and pulls, which is kinetic energy; it is pure information. It's connection; it's the culture that underlies all things.

This is our situation, and we have to make use of this. By entering upon a spiritual path, you can make better, easier use of it.

All evolution in the cosmos is based on this sudden pattern of development, which, when reaching the limits of a certain developmental stage, moves from one stage to the other through this sudden evolutionary leap. What Darwin was talking about was maintaining a biological species in the same shape. Mutations call for an internal state, and mutations cannot do this without a conscience. We have to make use of the inner resources.

We are presently at the bifurcation point, at the point of change, at the tipping point. This tipping point has two possible outcomes. Either they break down, which as I said is the BAU, or "business as usual," where everything will work the way it has worked and continue on. Then you have conflict and confrontation, eventually by military might, and also by economic, political, and cultural colonization, where people turn against one another, and there is escalating violence, terrorism, and war. That's the way to a breakdown.

The end of the world will not come at the end of 2012 as in the film.[1] It will come because we are destroying the balance on which our life depends, and we will notice that if people follow these lower paths, as the years pass, they will find it increasingly difficult to survive because of sea-level rise, increasing drought, reduced harvests, water pollution, and eruptions of violence. Entire populations will be flooded adding to the stress in the world. In a matter of years, we could have serious catastrophes, escalating eventually into extinction.

That's the negative scenario. We don't have to go to the negative scenario. We can shift to a positive scenario, from confrontation to dialogue, from violence to understanding, reinforce new cultures, the cultures of peace and nonviolence, the cultures of sustainability and move on to a level where we are creating communities, diverse communities that interact with one another, based on harmony and understanding.

Utopia? I tell you, it's a precondition of our survival. We cannot make it otherwise. We have too many people. We will destroy too much otherwise. We cannot just bounce around anymore. We have to consciously move to a harmonious worldwide civilization. As people recognize this as the only way, I am convinced that they will move. I just hope that they will do it in time, because all this has a time bomb. It has deadlines, which are not really deadlines but transformation lines, by which we need to change before the atmosphere heats up too much, before the waters of the sea flood, before clean water becomes unavailable to hundreds of millions of people, and poverty brings disease that becomes contagious.

We already have elemental change. We are not talking about something in the future. I have been talking about this change process now for maybe twenty years. Twenty years ago, people said, this is utopian. Now they see many communities looking for ways to live more responsibly, more sustainably, using global energy, recycling whenever they can, and communicating with others to reinforce that the quota of carbon does not exceed the living resources of the planet. This is a movement already underway, but it has to be fostered and encouraged.

It's a big project. It's a project of our civilization of renewal. This project is not unprecedented, because human civilization has moved through phases before. Obviously there is no time to talk about all the civilizations, but let me just talk about a few very briefly. For hundreds of thousands of years throughout the Stone Age, human civilization on the planet, which was mythological, was based on the idea that the whole world is alive and has a sacred dimension. In a dynamic universe, everything has meaning. Our ancestors can tell us, that the trees, the forest, the rivers, even storms, all have meaning and teach us something, and we can all live in harmony. Ask traditional people and indigenous people today how they look at the world, and they will give you this mythological worldview. Five thousand years ago, a big change occurred in the Middle East. Five thousand to two thousand years ago, gradually this change came about as a people formed an idea of the celestial sphere of the gods, how it is organized, and how this higher order could be used as guidance. They said, "Let's live by that here on earth." So, there are great theocratic Archaic Civilizations in Babylonia, Sumeria, Egypt, China, and India. These were different civilizations, no longer mythological in the Stone Age-sense, but instead trying to adapt themselves to the cosmic order of the sky gods.

Then came the Greeks. The Greeks were natural philosophers. They picked up these ideas and re-examined them in the light of reasoning. They said, let's organize and orient ourselves by reasoning out what is good. Aristotle was famous for his works, as was Plato in the various dialogues that spelled out the way human societies could organize themselves in a new principle of cooperation.

We don't have time to go into detail, but in the Middle Ages in Europe, this rationalistic way of thinking, this pure light of reason of the Greeks, mixed together with the theological elements from Christianity, Judaism, and Islam, and became the Medieval worldview, which was separated from practical reality when Galileo[2] and Giordiano Bruno[3] and others performed their famous experiments. But they made a covenant with the Catholic Church. They said that the church has the realm of human values, or what happens in society, the inner realm. Science examines the outer world, the world out there. What science examined based on the experiments of Galileo and the mathematics of Newton was a world made as a machine. You could explain it as if you could have levers in it, and causality like billiard balls pushing one another. So the entire world was conceived as a machine. Now, a machine doesn't have a soul, and a machine doesn't have consciousness. The machine is there to serve you. This was the mentality that developed, that nature exists to serve human interests. Because this mentality has been immensely successful in terms of developing technology and bigger power sources to create cities and transform the land, it has created a world that seems to fit human populations, but actually destroys the balance of the way nature operates, a nature which has a perfectly balanced system that has been operating for four billion years.

It's up to us now to make another step forward, not an unprecedented step but a logical step, and it is urgent that we take this step. These steps take hundreds of years. The Renaissance, the Reformation, and the rise to the Modern Age in the West took hundreds of years. It was a basic change from the medieval to the modern civilization. Now the modern civilization established many years ago has had its day. Now we have to move to the next step. This next step must intertwine science and spirituality. It must intertwine the mind and the body, and it must intertwine the individual and society, and society must intertwine with nature. It must be based on the concept that we live in a single spaceship, a natural spaceship, which is based on energy from the sun, with a certain given amount of material resources that need to be used carefully, recycled and reused as much as possible. If we pollute and destroy this spaceship, we all suffer. We will have exceeded the carrying capacity of our spaceship.

Why? Because we are changing the weather patterns, we are flooding many areas, we are polluting the water, and at least dozens of other reasons.

Here we have the need for a new holistic civilization. If you use the simple Greek terms, *methos, theos, lobos,* then we need to move to *holos,* a holistic civilization that doesn't destroy or disregard the others, but integrates knowledge into a new harmonious unity. What it does is change your values. It changes the way you look at yourself and the world.

I want to talk to you now about the values of inner consciousness. Because we have all of these problems before us, we need to co-create a new civilization. We are heating up the atmosphere. This has an impact on our health, on agriculture, on our forests, on our water, on the coastal areas, and all of the ecosystems. This is all evident. Let's just put it together. Climate change is already important, but now a whole series of new calculations have come about. The calculations show very clearly that a rise of two degrees average on the Celsius scale of temperature would create incredible difficulties for people to survive in the temperate zones. A rise of four degrees would make it impossible for more than a billion people to survive on this planet. We already are close to a critical threshold. The threshold is there, and it has become closer in the last million years. If we don't watch out, it could initiate a so-called runaway heat process. It's entirely possible. But we are not there yet and therefore, we still have time to make corrections.

The sea level will rise faster than has been predicted, because current measurements show that sea levels are rising faster than projections show. There are good reasons for it. The ice is melting at an enormous rate.

We are seeing on the one hand that salt water is rising, and on the other hand, the availability of fresh water is diminishing, while our population at the same time is still growing. These are unsustainable situations. The economic problems are just as serious as the ecological ones. This is why the current scenario of business as usual doesn't work.

I want to spend the remaining time talking about a new way of thinking. We can't solve these problems with the same kind of thinking. When you try to solve a problem of conflict among global nations by protecting them, what happens? You try to protect your interests by sending in the Marines, by using violence of any kind. When you try to overcome the problems of the financial system by just giving it more money, this deforms the system at the same time. We are just delaying the time for the next consciousness change. In all of these ways, it means that new values are necessary.

It means a new ethic. We all have our egocentric ethics. We can't expect that people will become totally altruistic and unselfish. Great saints and great prophets, yes, but most people remain accepting the basic values of the individual. Keep in mind, however, that individuals don't exist in a vacuum. Individuals have always lived as part of a community, and therefore, their search for individual satisfaction has always been mitigated by and integrated with the search for the values of its community.

A community is worldwide because what you do in one society affects other societies everywhere. When we look at our interests and ethics, we have to keep in mind that we are a global species. What is good for humanity must be what is good for us. If you conceive that something is good for us and bad for the human community, it is not really good for us either. It is thinking like cancer; if you keep reproducing you will break down the system.

A community also has to have a sociocentric ethic and have an eco-centric ethic because the planet, the biosphere as a whole, is our hope. This means basically a planetary ethic. I say a lot about this in my book, but just to point it out, this new ethic is an ethic of a planetary species, which is what we are. If we continue our tribal ethic, we will break down. Change has to come outside this level.

Then we have to get through all of these. There is a well-known saying of the famous physicist, Werner Heisenberg. He said the problem as physicists is not that we can't learn, the problem is that we can't forget. If you are changing to a new paradigm, this new paradigm is not due to the fact that leading scientists changed their minds; it is because the leading scientists died out. We have to discard obsolete ideas. It's not easy. But there is no longer time to wait for the dominant generation today to simply die out and hope that the next generation takes over. We must recognize what is obsolete about their thinking. Here are some examples.

One example is that the earth is an infinite source of resources. Another is that nature can be manipulated. It leads to genetic manipulation. Then there is the belief inaccurately ascribed to Darwin, because he didn't mean it that way, that life is a struggle, that the fittest survive. Life is not just a struggle for the survival of the fittest. Life must be aimed at making all people fit to survive, and this is a very different interpretation.

Today we have eight hundred individuals registered by the Fortune 500 indexes as being the richest people on earth. These eight hundred billionaires have an income equivalent to the income of about three billion people. Some people, some players, are much more powerful, and more aggressive.

They get much more benefit than the others, including competitors in the market that are eliminated, just pushed beyond the market. You cannot simply say, as long as I'm in the market, no matter what I do, if I benefit myself, I am going to benefit somebody else. The fact is, you have to create conditions under which the market can work. You have to create a social market where business competitors share control and orientation in the market, not just by legislation but with the competitors, business people, and clients and customers developing a different mentality. A lot can be said about that. The economy needs to be reformed and restructured.

Technology cannot solve all of our problems. It is a wrong belief that the old remedies will still work, where economic means are justified militarily. Underneath it all, war of any kind is suicidal. A new mentality is needed.

The worldview that dominates the world because it was born in the West and is now a global market is based on mechanistic production — a worldview that all things are separate and everyone is out for himself — nature being passive. This is very different from a worldview where everything is alive, where we are all in it together. Our economics, our culture, our ethos, everything needs to be reconsidered in this light.

It's easier for you now because you already have a different worldview. You are developing a worldview that co-originates dependency[4] of one thing with another. That's already a new worldview. This worldview in this case is the new worldview, and different from the typical worldview, which has a few people dominating mechanistically.

This worldview is good poetry, good art, good metaphysics, and good science.

November 9, 2009
SGI-USA New York Culture of Peace Resource Center

NOTES:

1. The film *2012* is an American science fiction disaster adventure film released in 2009.
2. Galileo Galilei (1564–1642) often known mononymously as Galileo was an Italian physicist, mathematician, engineer, astronomer, and philosopher who played a major role in the scientific revolution. Galileo's belief in the Copernican system eventually got him into trouble with the Catholic Church. The Inquisition was a permanent institution in the Catholic Church charged with the eradication of heresies. A committee of consultants declared to the Inquisition that the Copernican proposition that the sun is the center of the universe was a heresy. Because Galileo supported the Copernican system, he was warned by Cardinal

Bellarmine, under order of Pope Paul V, that he should not discuss or defend Copernican theories. In 1624, Galileo was assured by Pope Urban VIII that he could write about Copernican theory as long as he treated it as a mathematical proposition. However, with the printing of Galileo›s book, *Dialogue Concerning the Two Chief World Systems*, Galileo was called to Rome in 1633 to face the Inquisition again. Galileo was found guilty of heresy for his *Dialogue*, and was sent to his home near Florence where he was to be under house arrest for the remainder of his life. In 1638, the Inquisition allowed Galileo to move to his home in Florence, so that he could be closer to his doctors. By that time he was totally blind. In 1642, Galileo died at his home outside Florence.

3. Giordano Bruno (1548–1600) was an Italian Dominican friar, philosopher, mathematician, poet, and astrologer. He is celebrated for his cosmological theories, which went even further than the then novel Copernican model, proposing that the stars were just distant suns surrounded by their own exoplanets, and moreover, the possibility that these planets could even foster life of their own (a philosophical position known as cosmic pluralism). He also insisted that the universe is in fact infinite, thus having no celestial body at its "center."

4. The concept of dependent origination is a Buddhist doctrine expressing the interdependence of all things. It teaches that no beings or phenomena exist on their own; they exist or occur because of their relationship with other beings and phenomena. Everything in the world comes into existence in response to causes and conditions. That is, nothing can exist independent of other things or arise in isolation.

Creating a Space for the Disarmament Dialogue

The Pugwash Conferences

Jeffrey Boutwell

Executive Director
Pugwash Conferences on Science and World Affairs

Jeffrey Boutwell is the executive director of the Pugwash Conferences on Science and World Affairs.[1] Previously, he worked as the program director for international security studies at the American Academy of Arts and Sciences. He also served as a staff aide on the National Security Council during the Jimmy Carter administration. He is the author of *The German Nuclear Dilemma* and *The Nuclear Confrontation in Europe*.

Jeffrey Boutwell addresses several of the eight action areas defined in the 1999 United Nations Declaration and Programme of Action on a Culture of Peace, namely the eighth, promoting international peace and security.

Specifically addressing the abolition of nuclear weapons, Mr. Boutwell states, "If the United States and the other established nuclear powers could begin to devalue the currency of nuclear weapons, to diminish the role nuclear weapons have played in security policies for these many decades, we might create a new mindset where people don't witness the supposed prestige, either technical or political, that results from having nuclear weapons."

It's a pleasure to be here tonight. I can't resist starting with the recognition that today is Armistice Day; the eleventh hour of the eleventh day of the eleventh month in 1918, which signaled the end of "the war to end all wars." As we know, that was not to be the case. It's fitting that the snippet of the documentary film you saw about Joseph Rotblat, *Pugwash and Nuclear War*, ends with the Pete Seeger song, "Last Night I Had the Strangest Dream" about the end of wars. I have to tell you that, not only is the Pugwash Conferences on Science and World Affairs movement and the Pugwash organization dedicated to eliminating nuclear weapons, but it was part of Joseph Rotblat's credo that the abolition of war as a social institution had to be hand in hand with that. It was not enough just to get rid of the tools of violence; we had to get rid of the violence itself in whatever guise or form it might take — individual against individual, ethnic group against ethnic group, or nation state against nation state. Until we reach that, our work will only be half done.

If we get into a discussion later about the most feasible way to try and eliminate nuclear weapons, I will argue that they can be eliminated before war itself has been abolished. We have to, because as long as nuclear weapons exist, they will one day be used. That doesn't negate the importance of moving ahead institutionally, societally, psychologically and in whatever form we can, to abolish war as a social institution.

The film actively and wonderfully describes who Joseph Rotblat was as a person, the only scientist to voluntarily leave the Manhattan Project, when it was apparent that the Nazis were not going to acquire the bomb before the end of the European conflict. That was Joe's main motivation for having joined the Manhattan Project in the first place. He was Polish. He left Poland in August of 1939, shortly before the Nazis invaded. Unfortunately, his wife did not get out, and he never saw her again. He dedicated the rest of his war years to working with Britain and the United States on developing a nuclear weapon purely for deterrence purposes, should Hitler acquire it. When Hitler didn't develop the nuclear bomb technology, Joe left the Manhattan Project in December of 1944 and suffered for the rest of his life. He was subject to investigations by the U.S. House of Representatives Un-American Activities Committee in the 1950s. He was excoriated in the press. The FBI went through his belongings as they were shipped out of Los Alamos. From that time on, he was hounded and tainted by some as a traitor for having left the Manhattan Project.

If any of you have had the pleasure and honor of reading anything by

Joseph Rotblat, truly you have been in the presence of one of the world's great figures. I want to pay homage to the relationship that he and Mr. Daisaku Ikeda had for many years and the work that SGI and Pugwash did together in very different ways. I hope, in our conversation — and I do want to leave as much time for discussion and conversation as possible — that we can discuss tonight the different strategies by which these organizations have tried to eliminate nuclear weapons.

As the film mentioned and as we heard in the introduction, Pugwash works very much under the radar to bring together scientists, policy makers, and military officials for quiet meetings in the midst of partisan conflict with the Iranians, the Israelis and the Pakistanis, the Koreans, and the Chinese and the Japanese. We bring these folks together, creating a space for dialogue, much like the SGI does, but for scientists and policy makers to share ideas in a nonconfrontational forum. The purpose is for them to then take these ideas back to their governments to try and resolve the conflict scenarios and traps in which they find themselves.

We are not a public or grass-roots organization, and we don't try to stimulate and motivate public opinion per se in support of the goal of eliminating nuclear weapons. We are not set up like the People's Decade for Nuclear Abolition initiative. We don't have those types of tools, and frankly we don't have those types of resources; it's not what we do best. Other folks do that far better than we do. Nonetheless, I would posit that, if we are going to get to a world without nuclear weapons, we need public support. We need public support to not only push political leaders like Barack Obama, who has made this a centerpiece of his foreign policy, but see to it that important treaties are ratified, like the Comprehensive Nuclear-Test-Ban Treaty. If there is a fissile material treaty, that will need to be ratified. It's incredibly difficult to get the two-thirds vote in the U.S. Senate to approve any treaty. Across the political spectrum, we need to have the type of bipartisan support for these goals and initiatives that will come from public opinion.

I want to discuss with you and get ideas from you as to how organizations like the SGI or the Pugwash organization or others can bring these issues to the fore, because the reality is, and we all know it, nuclear weapons are not at the top of most people's agenda, in terms of what they worry about when they wake up every morning. They worry about and are most concerned with jobs, the economy, healthcare, climate change, and many other things much more immediate on the six o'clock news. How do we put this at the top of people's personal agendas? How do we tap into the anxiety and apprehension about the incredible devastation that nuclear weapons can cause so they work hard and tirelessly to eliminate them? How do we gain the support of leaders like Barack Obama?

I had a fascinating discussion with a group of young people before this evening's session. I want to emphasize a couple of points from that discussion. One is that political leadership can make a real difference. As you saw in the film, Mikhail Gorbachev played a central role in the 1980s to end the Cold War and dismantle the Iron Curtain that divided Europe, and by extension, make sure we did not enter into a World War III involving NATO and the Warsaw Pact. It took incredible political courage on his part to recognize that this was not a viable path for the Soviet Union. There has been much turmoil in Russia and the ex-Soviet states since then, but I would argue that they are far better off now and have a much better future than they did under the old Soviet regime. So Gorbachev played an incredibly important role.

So decisive political leadership can make a difference. In my own field of Middle East politics, I would say the same about Yitzhak Rabin, who took a tremendous risk for peace in 1992–93. We all know, unfortunately, that Yitzhak Rabin was assassinated by one of his countrymen and did not have the opportunity to put a peace process into place and Israeli domestic politics being what they are, things went south after Rabin was assassinated.

The other two leaders I have always admired are Anwar El Sadat and Menachem Begin. In the 1970s the Camp David Accords[2] achieved a breakthrough in the Israeli/Arab relations with the frameworks for Egyptian/Israeli normalization. As we know, in fact, Sadat paid for that with his life when he was assassinated in 1982.

Barack Obama has also made some important steps in that direction. His Prague speech in April of this year (2009) called for the goal of espousing a nuclear weapon free world. This is the first time a sitting U.S. president has ever done that. I mean, it's light years away from what even Bill Clinton was willing to say. I had a lot of hopes for Clinton in the 1990s at the end of the Cold War that weren't realized, but we won't get into that.

Barack Obama has come out with foursquare support of that goal, but he needs to do much more. It's easy to say that, but at the same time I recognize that he has many competing demands on his time, from pioneering change to healthcare reform to getting the economy back on track, to just reasserting a cooperative collective U.S. partnership with the rest of the world. He has got a lot of frayed ends to mend in terms of America's relations with countries around the world. If we're truly going to move this goal forward and eliminate nuclear weapons, however, Barack Obama does have to do a lot more.

One other thing we discussed earlier this evening with the students was going to Hiroshima. No sitting president has ever gone to Hiroshima or Nagasaki and made a speech about nuclear weapons. We're the only country that ever used them in wartime, and Japan is the only country that ever suffered from their use. How symbolic and how appropriate it would be for a president with great international credibility like Barack Obama to go to Hiroshima and Nagasaki to reiterate the goal of a nuclear weapon free world. The United States is both a country with the moral responsibility for having used them in war, and the preeminent nuclear power in the world. If we're going to take the lead — take a combination of unilateral steps but also work with the Russians, the Chinese, the French, and the British, as the original nuclear weapon states — to begin to greatly reduce nuclear weapon stockpiles and put things in place like the Comprehensive Nuclear-Test-Ban Treaty, or other nonproliferation measures of no first-use policy, it will take that kind of galvanizing, clarity, and calm on the part of the sitting U.S. president to galvanize public opinion both in this country and around the world.

Pugwash started out as an organization primarily of scientists and physicists, people who worked on the respective bomb programs during World War II. Since then, it has expanded greatly. We now have chapters in more than fifty countries around the world, and we have as many if not more policy experts, military leaders, even business people, in Pugwash as we do scientists. Frankly, the nuclear weapon problem is no longer a scientific and technical problem like it was in the 1950s and 1960s. Back then there was still much uncertainty about radiation effects and circular aero-blast effects. We know that nuclear weapons are truly a genocidal or homicidal weapon and, if they are ever used, they will be indiscriminate and will, in my mind, fall fully under the U.N. Convention on genocide. I think whoever uses them should be prosecuted for crimes against humanity and nuclear radiation and genocide. If a nuclear weapon is not genocide, what is?

Pugwash has expanded its agenda. In the fifty-two years that we have been in operation, it has expanded its participant base. We work in regions of conflict, as I mentioned before, with Iranians, Israelis, Pakistanis, Indians, in places where the risk of conflict is at its highest and where nuclear weapons are present and could be used. And we work under the radar. We had a series of fascinating meetings last year involving Mojtaba Samareh Hashemi, a senior advisor to President Ahmadinejad of Iran, in Europe over a series of four occasions with top U.S. officials, including Bill Perry and others. These meetings occurred totally out of the limelight, just as a back channel way of trying to make the Iranian and U.S. views of the nuclear impasse more transparent.

Since then, domestic politics being what they are both in Iran and the United States, we haven't made much progress. I'm afraid we won't until the power struggle going on within Iran sorts itself out. It's tough to tell for sure, as Iranian politics are not easy to decipher even for the experts, but until that sorts itself out, we're going to probably be in a stalemate in terms of resolving the Iranian issue.

At least for its part, Pugwash continues to create the space for dialogue, to create the venues for people to come together to exchange their views and make their views better known to the other side. As we talked about in our session before this meeting, generating support from the domestic public for military expenditures and the continued role of nuclear weapons requires the demonization of the enemy. It happens between India and Pakistan, it happens between Israel and Iran, and it happens between North Korea and the outside world. One participant in our earlier discussion made a very valid point that nuclear weapons and demonizing the United States as the boogeyman is probably the only legitimacy the North Korean regime has to keep a hold on its people. Certainly, they don't provide the necessities of life or social cohesion or anything else, but as long as they can scare their populace into thinking that the United States might attack them one day, ergo, we need nuclear weapons to deter such an attack. That's one way they stay in power.

If the United States and the other established nuclear powers could begin to devalue the currency of nuclear weapons, to diminish the role nuclear weapons have played in security policies for these many decades, we might create a new mindset where people don't witness the supposed prestige, either technical or political, that results from having nuclear weapons. We also have to do some fundamental rearranging of the international politics. It's no longer credible that the five permanent members of the U.N. Security Council are the five original nuclear weapon states. How can you argue that France or Britain deserve a seat on the Security Council when countries like Indonesia, South Africa, Brazil, Japan, and Germany do not? It's all based on nuclear weapons and having nuclear weapons. So we need new ways to resolve disputes, adjudicate disputes in the United Nations, and end violence between countries. For its part, Pugwash Conferences work below the radar to bring people together, but it's going to take more public support as well, and that's where groups and organizations like the SGI play such an important role.

November 11, 2009
SGI-USA Washington, D.C., Culture of Peace Resource Center

NOTES:

1. Jeffrey Boutwell was executive director of the International Pugwash Conferences from 1997 to 2010. Currently he serves as the secretary of the U.S. Pugwash.
2. On September 17, 1978, Israel and Egypt signed two agreements, the first between Israel and any of its Arab neighbors. The Camp David Accords were negotiated by the Israeli Prime Minister Menachem Begin and the Egyptian President Anwar El Sadat under the mediation of U.S. President Jimmy Carter at the government retreat at Camp David, Maryland. The peace treaty that Israel and Egypt eventually signed on March 26, 1979, closely reflected the Camp David Accords.

The Role of Religion in
Building Civil Society

Patrick James

Professor of International Relations and Director of
the Center for International Studies
The University of Southern California

Patrick James is professor of international relations and director of the Center for
International Studies at the University of Southern California. Mr. James has a PhD
from the University of Maryland and specializes in comparative and international
politics. His interests at the international level include the causes, processes, and consequences of conflict, crisis, and war. Mr. James is the author of fourteen books and
more than one hundred articles and book chapters. Among his honors and awards are
the Louise Dyer Peace Fellowship from the Hoover Institution at Stanford University,
the Milton R. Merrill Chair from Political Science at Utah State University, the Lady
Davis Professorship of the Hebrew University of Jerusalem, the Thomas Enders Professorship in Canadian Studies at the University of Calgary, the Senior Scholar award
from the Canadian Embassy, Washington, D.C., the Eaton Lectureship at Queen's University in Belfast. He is a past president of the Midwest International Studies Association and the Iowa Conference of Political Scientists. Mr. James has been recognized
as a Distinguished Scholar in Foreign Policy Analysis for the International Studies
Association, 2006-07. He served as vice president, 2005-07, and president, 2007-
09, of the Association for Canadian Studies in the United States, and vice president
(2008-09) of the ISA. Mr. James also served a five-year term as editor of the *International Studies Quarterly*.

> Patrick James touches on many of the eight action areas
> in the 1999 United Nations Declaration and Programme of
> Action on a Culture of Peace, especially the sixth: advancing
> understanding, tolerance, and solidarity. As Mr. James says:
> "Think about what the word *tolerance* means — I tolerate
> you or you tolerate me. It doesn't sound that appealing
> does it? You're putting up with me, so to speak. As a form
> of tolerance, respect is more active, and the sooner you

get people to open their minds and move beyond mere toleration toward respect, that's when you get over the hump, when their religiosity, their faith, helps to grease the wheels toward bridging with other groups. Their religious faith, rather than being an obstacle in this context, facilitates their moving in a more positive direction than before."

I will speak tonight about the role of religion in building civil society. My purpose is to explore the concept of social capital and the accumulation of social capital as a potentially positive product of religious identity. The RIGG project stands for Religion, Identity, and Global Governance. It's a very large-scale project, and I am going to speak today about a part of the RIGG agenda that directly connects with this lecture series. There will be an abstract discussion and then I am going to get into the applications part.

For those who want to know more about the first three years of the RIGG project, there was a book published by the University of Toronto Press in 2010. I originally hail from Canada and take pride in the fact that Canada has a strong tradition of peacekeeping and peacebuilding known around the world. The Canadian University presses are more favorable to this type of research, so there tends to be an overrepresentation of peacebuilding-oriented publications with presses like the University of Toronto, the combined McGill-Queen's University, and the University of British Columbia. Our book will be the latest attempt at contributing to that area.

I think, among the goals of the SGI-USA Culture of Peace Distinguished Speaker Series, my talk will relate to the goal of advancing understanding, tolerance, and solidarity; it would be fair to say that my talk will have some relevance to the other goals of the series, but this is the goal you want to keep in the back of your mind as I move through the discussion. We are trying to say things that are constructive and helpful along those lines.

Religion is a double-edged sword. The events of 9/11 were horrific, both on that day, and arguably for much of the aftermath they have created, for the decade that has followed. It was violent; it was destructive. It became associated in the public mind with other destructive and violent actions attributed to radical Islam and, to be very careful about how I say this, to radical Islamists, not to people of the Islamic faith proper. That is an important distinction to make throughout our discussion. Now there is another edge to the sword of religion in general, and you might say, allowing a weak pun, the scimitar of Islam in particular. Religion can do positive and constructive things. Of course, here we are together gathered at the SGI, that would seem to overstate the obvious, but once you go outside this building, there are a lot of people who don't see it that way, who do not see religion as anything other than destructive and irrational, whether it's radical Islamists taking out buildings with airplanes or people from other religious faiths claiming to be in those faiths and doing violent destructive things on their behalf. The focus today is going to be on some very positive and constructive activities identified with religion that contribute to peacebuilding, cooperation, and human solidarity.

Social capital is the concept I am working with today. What is it? James Coleman was a sociologist, who, from the 1970s onward, worked on sociological concepts. He deserves an enormous amount of credit for thinking through the metaphor of capital accumulation from economics. I do not mean to slight others who played essential roles in developing the concept of social capital, but in this talk I'll reference him most directly.

So we hear from economists, with regard to their domain, that we need to accumulate capital to get investment going and to get people back to work. The metaphor by the great sociologist, Coleman, is that in our society we might have an analog, we might have something that we call social capital. Instead of piles of money that might be sitting in banks, it is measured in terms of group formation and solidarity within society. For example, how many social organizations does a society have? How cohesive are those organizations? That's what social capital is about.

Robert Putnam from Harvard University has been the main exponent of social capital among those studying political processes, so political scientists, and people interested in conflicts, perhaps even religious conflicts, have been interested in his books on this subject over the last twenty years or so. He is generally credited with the main definition that people who study politics tend to use, namely that, "Social capital refers to the collective value of all social networks and the inclinations that arise from these networks to do things for each other."

Take a moment and read that again. It's a sense of capital accumulation in society as opposed to within the economy. What groups are out there and how well are they working with one another? Are there social networks, and so on and so forth.

In economics, we know that capital accumulation is important in order for companies to have money to invest, to employ people, and to get things moving forward. Who cares about this stuff? We do, because it ends up being very important to how societies function. There are two kinds of social capital — bonding capital and bridging capital. I am going to introduce these variations and show their importance; I am going to link them with things we're very concerned about, major issues of public policy.

Bonding capital refers to people doing things in groups, such as bowling leagues or clubs that have some kind of exclusive membership. With organizations like Rotary, for instance — you can't just join Rotary, you have to be invited. There are other organizations we could mention, for example, people who collect stamps. Putnam actually became famous by looking at bowling leagues; he took note of the decline of bowling leagues as social organizations.

His famous book is called *Bowling Alone*. People generally now go bowling in very small groups that are not organized in any way — they are not a formal network; they are not a bowling league; or they just go by themselves. He noticed this and looked at other kinds of social organizations in the United States. This spawned a tremendous amount of controversy later on as to whether people doing things alone, like watching TV or getting on the Internet, whether it was killing social organization in the United States. So one basic group is the so-called bonding group, where people bond together to do something; they have a purpose of one sort or another. The membership, and this is important to remember, is exclusive.

Bridging capital are groups anybody can join. An example of a famous one in American history is the National Association for the Advancement of Colored People (NAACP). From its founding, the NAACP played an important role in the struggle against racism in American society, more than maybe any other group you can think of. The NAACP wanted everyone to join, if at all possible. They didn't care what color you were or what language you might have learned growing up, or what your religion was; it was designed to advance the interests of people who had experienced oppression within American society.

Bridging capital, such as that created by an organization like the NAACP, is valuable because it reaches across social networks. Think about this; this might be a good way to keep it in your mind as I progress. Bonding capital is like islands; bridging capital is like bridges, enabling people on the islands to communicate and cooperate with one another. Bonding capital on its own can become very bad news, but in conjunction with bridging capital, it can make a society function more effectively with more positive results.

Next, we have the late and awful Timothy McVeigh, responsible for the bombing attack in Oklahoma City in 1995. He is a counterexample of where you have bonding capital, a small group of individuals, in this case, who were like-minded, who hated the government and many of their fellow citizens, and who practiced a sort of warped or even demented form of Christianity, akin to what we might call radical Islamism — violence and exclusivity. We don't want that sort of thing proliferating, right?

We want to see the islands of bonding capital effectively bridge together to create greater cooperation than they have so far exhibited. To take an extreme example, try to imagine cooperation between members of SeanHannity.com on the one hand and Moveon.org on the other. Moveon.org, of course, is identified with Michael Moore. Everybody knows Sean Hannity, right? What would these two have in common in terms of membership? I would submit that anybody who belonged to both would be either a spy for one or terribly confused, because they have no common interest.

They can't work together because they disagree so much. What we would enjoy in this fantasized example is to see them cooperate on something. Wouldn't that be good for American society, whether you happen to be a liberal or a conservative, or whatever in between? That would almost have to be good. That's my argument. Such extreme groups make my argument form even more powerfully, because they are the toughest to get to work together. Many other groups might have more potential for mobilization for a good cause.

Social capital now in a religious context — some people might ridicule Putnam and bonding capital, bridging capital, and all I have been talking about and say, "What a waste of time, because these group identifications are not that powerful and you can't mobilize people around stamp collecting or bowling; what on earth are you talking about?" Ah hah! What does make sense is to zero in on religious affiliation. It's a more intense form of affiliation, and it could be a significant basis for building both kinds of social capital within a society.

For instance, I will give you a couple of examples. You could measure in terms of church membership and participation how much bonding capital exists in a society; you could use these as crude indicators. Extreme cases of bonding capital in action might include McVeigh-like violence, but what if you can get the groups together? What if you could move them away from extremism and toward cooperation? Also, we sometimes see bridging capital in the most surprising cases. About fifteen years ago, there were twin earthquakes in Greece and Turkey. Both sides, despite having had great differences with each other — in the Aegean Sea and principally over sovereignty on Cyprus with Greek Orthodox on the one hand and Islam on the other — they engaged in extraordinary acts of generosity back and forth, and shocked the world in a positive way. This would be a dramatic example of bridging capital — cooperation. More of that almost has to be good by definition, doesn't it?

Concerning ourselves with bonding and bridging capital is all very nice, but who cares? It is a nice thing to see them cooperate with each other. What we do know is that, when bonding and bridging capital are measured at high levels, a very nice and powerful effect takes place that has implications for all kinds of public policies, namely, the building of trust. The research done by academics on the subject shows that, if you have a proliferation of bonding and bridging capital together, it warrants social networking of both kinds. There is a lot of it out there that tends to be associated with getting over the hump in a society to where people trust one another more, toward them cooperating when they are not in a particular group or dealing with somebody that they happen to know.

What kinds of things are going on? What are some examples that might interest us because we have some interest perhaps in faith-based organizations and what they can do for peacebuilding. We are getting there; we're getting closer.

Some religiously oriented examples are connected to the building of bridging capital, and by implication, the improvement of civil society and the building of trust. The IGE or the Institute for Global Engagement is a good example. It is absolutely fascinating to see what Chris Seiple and his organization are all about and what they are doing.

They are very much behind the scenes and are low-key. They are building what I am calling bridging capital. It is a religious freedom organization that works with all faiths in the most difficult places in the world. If you go to their website (globalengage.org), the IGE will recount what they are doing in Laos, Vietnam, and Pakistan for those who study religious conflict, or just have some awareness of where the hot spots are in the world.

They are deliberately picking some of the most dangerous and challenging locations to work in. The IGE will build mutual respect right on the ground among religious groups, which in turn can build cooperation and improve society, civil society, that is, through this so-called bridging capital. They will perhaps get an Imam together with a Christian leader, or maybe from some other group that has been fighting, and they will bring people together and they will try to bridge.

I talked to Chris Seiple about this, and I collaborated with him because he is also a trained academic with a PhD. He said something absolutely fascinating about the first thing he does when he gets leaders together, perhaps in a Laotian village where there has been a lot of fighting and violence.

Does anybody know the first thing he does when they finally agree to sit down? What does he do? Anybody want to guess? Prayer! They are taken aback and surprised that he doesn't offer them a meal; he also doesn't offer them a drink. Instead he asks if they would like to pray, each according to their own tradition. What he is getting them to do is build a bridge into one another's mind so they seem less alien. At that moment, the other person isn't shooting a gun at me, or trying to stab me; they are doing something analogous to what I do; they are expressing their religious faith.

He has a brilliant mind and is very insightful. The techniques he uses are not manipulative; they are honest and direct. He gets people to think about their positions. His work is much like pushing a rock up a steep hill, but you will find few people who have as much patience as he does. I use this as an example because, when I tried to think about how to connect with an audience interested in the SGI and its programming, I realized that this is peacebuilding from the ground up. This is honoring the traditions an organization like the SGI supports, working honestly and openly with people, trying to get them to think creatively about peace. I think the IGE is a great example of an effort to build mutual respect among groups that, let's face it, had not been respecting one another, let alone, in some cases, even allowing one another to live side by side.

Another example is Robert Lloyd, a political scientist at Pepperdine University, who wrote a wonderful chapter where he looks at "track 2 mediation" efforts by Christian organizations, so this focuses on the Christian side of things. Track 2 is a nickname given in diplomatic studies for "below the top level." Track 1 is when our secretary of state talks to his or her equivalent somewhere or even when President Obama is representing the United States at an organization. Track 2 means those who are mid-level and can more freely express their ideas without worrying about a quote ending up on the front page of *The New York Times*. It gives them freedom to say what they want to say. They can make a concession, put forward an idea, or throw out something without risk. He focuses on these creative buildups toward breakthroughs in peace, tracked through styled mediation efforts. These are attempts to manage or even eliminate destructive conflict in society.

The most famous example is the South African Truth and Reconciliation Commission. How many of you knew it was established by Methodist and Anglican church leaders? Out of curiosity, how many people knew that? One person in the back, that's what I usually get from audiences, a small percentage of people. Notice the interesting experiment we just did. Everybody knows about 9/11 and everybody knows about the Khobar Towers and the *USS Cole*, and all the bloodshed, but what about the more positive stories that involve religion? Think about the attention they don't get. A positive story like that in South Africa is at the high end of visibility, and yet we still didn't know much about the religious component. This came, of course, after the end of apartheid and democratization in the mid-90s, and it is not that long ago that people forgot; I think that it was just overlooked.

Here is a case I suspect is even lesser known, but just as important and interesting in its own way because it looked hopeless at the outset. I am talking about a case in Mozambique relative to the Community of Sant'Egidio, a lay public association of the Catholic Church. Jaime Goncalves is the key pivotal player here. This organization played an extremely important and major role in mediating an end to a violent and destructive civil war in Mozambique. In the early 1990s, Goncalves, the Roman Catholic Archbishop of Beira, together with members of the Sant'Egidio group, started a dialogue with the leadership of the rebel National Resistance Movement of Mozambique (RENAMO). The RENAMO movement was opposed to the sort of quasi-Marxist far-left government in charge of Mozambique at the time. It was very violent and confrontational; lots of people were killed.

In October 1992, the Community of Sant'Egidio negotiated the Rome General Peace Accord with the support of the United Nations. It was signed in Rome between Mozambique President Joaquim Chissano and the RENAMO leader, and it formally took effect on October 15 of that year. It's a very happy story.

I am going to do another experiment. How many in the room, even if they knew about the Mozambique civil war settlement, knew about the significant religious mediation that took place? This time, zero! I am an international relations specialist, and I've been in this field for thirty years, so guess what? I did not put up my hand either and, until I read Robert Lloyd's research on the subject, I did not know this either. If someone who does this for a living doesn't know, it essentially shows us the bias out there. We are not thinking about the positive role religion plays, so we tend to miss it. It is similar to when my wife suffers tremendous frustration in my inability to find things in our refrigerator. After fourteen years of marriage, I still struggle with this. I know that is a trivial case to use, but we are not thinking about the positive role of religion and, even if we individually are people of faith, we are not thinking about that role. We are missing it, and it is out there to be found.

Mediation does not always work as well as those two cases. It is raining outside, so let me drop some rain on us, figuratively speaking. It doesn't work a lot of the time; however, it is hard to know how much worse things might have been without religious mediation. So you have some clear successes, like the two I mentioned, but you have other cases where, at the very least, religious mediators may have played an important holding action; people who might have been dead otherwise are not. It's hard to measure that but it's there. It's there to some degree; it's just tough to measure.

Let me return to my abstractions. The building of bridging capital is what you do when you mediate between groups who previously have been out to kill each other because of their religious briefs. You're creating the foundation for bridging capital and for more trust, greater understanding, tolerance, and even solidarity. That's the sector I am talking about the most today; that's the goal I am zeroing in on. In the successful cases, the most successful cases, you can even say that some degree of solidarity is built between and among previous enemies. Religious organizations can have a major and positive role to play in these things through so-called track 2 diplomacy.

Now I would like to speak about linking up directly with some priorities from the SGI. For example, I want to start with the Declaration of Principles on Tolerance from UNESCO on November 16, 1995. It's very important for me to link my abstract concepts to the real world, so I am triangulating some ideas from the United Nations.

The key point in my mind with this document from November 1995 is what appears in that document's Article 1, Subsection 1.1. "Tolerance is respect." That's a direct quotation. When you look at the work religious mediators do, they do not emphasize the word *tolerance* for long, instead, they try by sleight of hand to say, "Let's go to respect as quickly as we can." Think about what the word *tolerance* means — I tolerate you or you tolerate me. It doesn't sound that appealing does it? You're putting up with me, so to speak. As a form of tolerance, respect is more active, and the sooner you get people to open their minds and move beyond mere toleration toward respect, that's when you get over the hump, when their religiosity, their faith, helps to grease the wheels toward bridging with other groups. Their religious faith, rather than being an obstacle in this context, facilitates their moving in a more positive direction than before.

Consider also that the UNESCO Constitution wasn't written by a bunch of college professors studying social capital, but notice that some of this language is being used indirectly. Let me link with that Article 4 from the Declaration of Principles on Tolerance that emphasizes education in Subsection 4.3: "Education for tolerance should aim at countering influences that lead to fear and exclusion of others, and should help young people to develop capacities for independent judgment, critical thinking, and ethical reasoning," and here are the key words, "exclusion of others." Another way of saying that is maybe for UNESCO to call for the building of bridging organizations as opposed to just bonding organizations, as in "me and my friends, the rest of you keep out." I think that language is embedded and implicit. I could give you more examples but we would be here all night. I could quote chapter and verse from plenty of other analogs or parallels with my initial academic treatment inside these UNESCO and other U.N. documents.

UNESCO is opening the door to the idea of tolerance as respect, as advocated by the IGE. My other example is the U.N. Declaration and Programme of Action on a Culture of Peace from September 13, 1999. What is that all about? Section B.a3, etc., is a very intricate document. It took me a while to work through its intricacies, but I learned a lot.

"Civil society should be involved at the local, regional, and national levels to widen the scope of activities on a culture of peace."

Let me read out the other quote and then I am going to link them together and make an analysis.

"Support actions that foster understanding, tolerance, solidarity, and cooperation among peoples and within and among nations." That, if you dissect it and put it back together, sounds a lot like tolerance as respect intended to bridge previously exclusive groups within and across national borders. What tends to be more exclusive and divisive than national borders? Immediately, maybe we think, put a border somewhere, put up some barbed wire, some people with machine guns, or whatever the case may be, or at the very least, somebody who asks you for your passport and demands to know why you are coming in. That's the mindset of bridging capital, where you break down barriers and encourage people to think through them and over them rather than about them.

I would like to bring together another concept with those I have been building on so far. If you could build bridging capital — and now we know what this is and how it might be pursued in a religious context — you could improve trust. Remember that academic research teaches this. I don't have time to get into everything that is a building block, but massive support exists on that particular point: that bridging capital facilitates trust, and that good public policy implications come from trusting versus non-trusting societies.

Civil society is improved by that and the results are then transferrable across borders, because if you have more trusting societies within national borders, the likelihood is that they can cooperate across those borders more effectively into, what is often called these days, "global governance." What we need, while living in this world of globalization, is to improve the way the world is collectively managed so that our grandchildren and their grandchildren will have something to live on by the time they get here. All of this then becomes very important. It isn't just a series of abstractions or discussions from textbooks; it is a mechanism to improve the world in which we live.

I'll share some conclusions now. There is another edge, as I was saying at the beginning of this talk, to the sword of religion. It can be used to cut what looks like Gordian knots, unbreakable knots out there that perpetuate conflict and inspire fanatical killers. Because, if you strike up a casual conversation with someone who is not politically aware, not attending public events of this nature, and not broadly educated in these areas, they will tell you in a matter-of-fact manner that religion generally gets people killed. That's what it does. That is a regrettably common one-sided perception that is out there, but it could do other things.

I've shared with you a few examples, but there are many other examples, not just Christian examples. There are other groups I could focus on, but I wanted to present some examples to you, those that are straightforward.

For the IGE and the Christian mediation group, Sant'Egidio, bridging capital paved the way for reconciliation. Bridging capital builds greater trust in a civil society, and therefore the potential for improved global governance, so we should care about this argument. If this argument is right, it's downright exciting because it is a mechanism for people to do positive things beyond, say, voting, which might affect who gets elected. There are other ways to affect positive change, and this is one of them.

The U.N. goals are linked to the mandate of the SGI as an organization; these goals, when I delved into them and gave you examples, sound like they are reading the same books I am. Their language is somewhat different, but the logic and the argument look remarkably similar upon inspection, at least to me.

All the major religions — and I want to emphasize this point — and even the minor religions with a few adherents can participate in this. No religion with a significant following around the world is inconsistent with this kind of cooperation. They all have at least some doctrinal statements that support this type of cooperative venture. It will be a great challenge, however, to overcome the much more prominent and infamous forms of division. I gave you some rather ugly pictures at the beginning about that. We could have talked about some elements of the past in Christianity and Judaism that people would not be proud of even today, but all of the religions have this potential to do something positive in tandem with one another.

Now my question for you is: How might the SGI or other organizations fit into all this? How might you as an individual find this interesting? By the way, if I need to encourage it, where are the holes in all of this? I care very deeply about whether this is right. It's not just about an academic book and who might read it. It's also about whether this mechanism makes sense, if this is a path to greater peace, to a better life for people.

December 12, 2009
SGI-USA Santa Monica Culture of Peace Resource Center

Engaging Women as Peacebuilders

Carla Koppell

Director
The Institute for Inclusive Security

Carla Koppell is the director of The Institute for Inclusive Security, which uses research, training, and advocacy to promote the inclusion of women in global, sustainable peacemaking efforts. She received her master's in public policy from Harvard University's Kennedy School of Government in Cambridge, Massachusetts, and her bachelor's of science from Cornell University in Ithaca, New York.

During her tenure at the Institute for Inclusive Security, Ms. Koppell worked extensively with leaders from volatile conflict zones around the world including Afghans, Colombians, Iraqis, Israelis, Liberians, Palestinians, South Sudanese, and Sudanese.

Earlier in her career, Ms. Koppell was senior adviser and, prior to that, interim director of the Conflict Prevention Project at the Woodrow Wilson International Center for Scholars in Washington, D.C., where she authored "Preventing the Next Wave of Conflict: Understanding Non-Traditional Threats to Global Stability." Ms. Koppell served as deputy assistant secretary for international affairs of the United States Department of Housing and Urban Development (HUD), helping steward bilateral relationships with South Africa, China, and Israel in addition to overseeing HUD contributions to Central America and the Caribbean reconstruction following Hurricanes Mitch and Georges She also directed the USAID climate change program and, earlier in her career, worked for the Food and Agriculture Organization of the United Nations.

Carla Koppell touches on many of the eight action areas defined in the 1999 United Nations Declaration and Programme of Action on a Culture of Peace, most notably the fourth, ensuring equality between women and men, and the eighth, promoting international peace and security.

In her lecture on the topic of women in international peace negotiations, Ms. Koppell states: "Broadly speaking, there are fundamental flaws in the way peace is constructed around the world. The key fundamental flaw is in the way the peace processes are actually built — the way they are constructed and the way they are put together.

"The U.N. Development Fund for Women recently published a study that found less than 5 percent of the signatories to peace agreements are women.

"But, where women have been involved, the content of the peace agreements and the nature of the negotiations themselves have changed. So you see differences in terms of the substance, and you see differences in terms of the process.

"Women put the provisions into those agreements stating that, when combatants were demobilized, efforts needed to be made that dealt not only with getting those people back into society, but also provided for their education, healthcare, and retraining. These women took a good, hard look into the provisions and inserted their requests into the negotiated accord."

It is a rare privilege to speak to members of an organization founded and led by men like Tsunesaburo Makiguchi and Daisaku Ikeda who appreciate women as builders of peace and the key to enabling a culture of peace.

The Institute for Inclusive Security, which I direct, is dedicated to bringing other stakeholders into the peace process. While we focus particularly on bringing women into the process, we recognize that there are other stakeholders who care equally about peace who are often not brought into the conversation.

Broadly speaking, there are fundamental flaws in the way peace is constructed around the world. The key fundamental flaw is in the way the peace processes are actually built — the way they are constructed and the way they are put together.

Today most peace processes are secret and selective, involving a narrow cross section of the population in a closed process invisible to many of the stakeholders who have a role and an interest in peace.

Imagine for a minute: If you were creating a peace process, who would you want to have involved? Wouldn't you want those with an investment in peace, with an investment in security, with an investment in safety, those most committed to a culture of peace? And yet today, almost universally, the only people brought together to negotiate peace are the warriors — those who have taken up arms to get their voices heard as opposed to those who have refused to take up arms and still seek to be heard.

Peace processes are not being set up in a way that will create proper incentives conducive to peace, and that enable a long-term spirit of reconciliation. What I mean is, often peace processes result in an end to hostilities, in an end to gunfire. But the likelihood that that process results in long-term peace, prosperity, stability, and a real culture of peace, as we would call it, are often very slim.

Perhaps the best way to think about this, before I speak about women's inclusion in the peace process, would be to share a few anecdotes.

At one peace process, when I talked to those at the table, all men, I said: "Why don't you have any women involved? Women are probably the majority of your population at this point, after years and years of conflict, so why aren't there any women here?" The men responded: "Why would we bring women? They would just compromise."

It's the context of negotiation ... but OK.

At another peace process, I worked with Darfurian women — women who, after the sixth round of negotiations, had been finally included and finally given a voice. I said to these women: "Would it make a difference, or, does it matter if you are here or not?"

These women replied: "Well, you know the agenda was already set up for the negotiation. The top two issues were, how do we divide up power and how do we divide up wealth. If *we* were there, our key concern would be, how to get security back on the ground. So, in terms of what we're looking for even in the dialogue process, our priorities are completely different, reflected not only in the dialogue but in the agenda for peace — our priority would be that security matters."

So as these anecdotes reveal, not as definitive proof, but as a good indicator of the kinds of challenges that are faced in the structure of the peace process today, I would like to pose two questions.

First, would it make a difference in the peace process for others to be involved? Is there evidence of this? I am, after all, just relaying two stories and they don't necessarily relate to the result of the negotiations.

Second, why is it so hard to change? If the premise is self-evident that you need to have other players in the process, why aren't we moving quickly to change the way the structures are put in place?

In regard to my first question — would it make a difference — I would say yes, it would. The evidence and documentation that this is the case is increasingly obvious where women are involved. Parenthetically, I will say that having women involved is extremely rare. A UNIFEM (U.N. Development Fund for Women) recently published a study that found less than 5 percent of the signatories to peace agreements are women.

But, where women have been involved, the content of the peace agreements and the nature of the negotiations themselves have changed. So you see differences in terms of the substance, and you see differences in terms of the process.

Women add key issues to agreements. In Northern Ireland women were seated at the negotiating table, while in most peace processes, women play a more indirect role. But in Northern Ireland, they had a direct role.

At the end of the Northern Ireland peace process negotiations, which were relatively successful, women had included provisions for things like unified education. But in places like Bosnia, unified education was not an outcome of their peace process. The women in Northern Ireland felt that having a uniform system for educating youth was the key to the long-term rebuilding and reconciling of their society and would ensure that everyone shared a common view of history, one accepted by both sides in the negotiation process.

In Uganda, looking at the changes made in the negotiated agreement and determining whether the women involved influenced the decisions, you can see that the women would have made sure that the ceasefire included not only putting down weapons, but also a call for a cessation of the sexual violence.

Women put the provisions into those agreements stating that, when combatants were demobilized, efforts needed to be made that dealt not only with getting those people back into society, but also provided for their education, healthcare, and retraining. These women took a good, hard look into the provisions and inserted their requests into the negotiated accord.

In Sudan and Darfur, a full agreement has not yet been determined, but one has been negotiated with one of the three rebel groups through the Darfur Peace Agreement. In this instance, women have placed provisions into the agreement to ensure that wealth-sharing for female-headed households and for women in general was included so that female-headed households in this quite conservative society could obtain property and secure jobs and move their families forward in the post-conflict period.

Now it's interesting to note, in almost all of these cases, and in fact, in all the ones I've mentioned, the substance of what those women put into the agreement was noncontroversial. No one was upset that those provisions were included, nor were those provisions necessarily debated in any heated way. What that means is that women were putting forward items that were forgotten because their interests were not being represented at the negotiation table, and they were inserting noncontroversial items.

Why is that important in the context of negotiation? It's important because often you're looking for that thread of commonality that will provide the foundation for broader negotiation. You need to find something you can agree on to get the ball rolling. And in many cases, the women provided just that. They provided the space to move the dialogue forward among a group of warriors into a positive place, thereby creating the groundwork for a broader agreement.

Another important point about what these women added to the process is that their requests often provided a space for everyone to take a long, hard look at what was needed to reinstitute peace and prosperity, the very culture of peace that was supposed to be framed within the construct of the negotiating process — important things that would have been left out if the women had not been there.

Third, the women focused on creating connections with the citizens. As I mentioned earlier, most negotiations are exclusive, secretive, and closed. There is little communication with the citizens living in the area. The meetings are usually held in a third location, a location not involved in the conflict so as to offer a perceived neutrality, which is fine. But it also means that there is a disconnect from the people who need to buy into and implement that agreement.

These women care about creating local ownership. If you look at the peace agreements in Guatemala, in Uganda, and in other places around the world, women are the ones who verbalize the need to create a loop back to the people living there so they know what is happening. Foreign negotiations that go on for years without communication with the local citizens are not creative recipes for success. Those lines of communication need to be established.

It is these women who say, we're going back, we need to talk to our constituencies. Often these women are actually from the communities, not some leaders based elsewhere, who engage in the negotiating process and want to communicate with the people living in the conflict areas. They provide that link back to the local population that needs to buy into the negotiated process and move it forward.

Fourth, women are improving the foundation for long-term reconciliation and for reconstruction. They're doing both because they have these constituencies locally, because they're providing the connection back to civil society, and because they are often the ones who provide the services within those communities.

In Afghanistan during the Taliban period, it was often the women who provided the healthcare and education even in the war zones. By bringing women into the dialogue around a peace process, it brought in the people being asked to implement the programs — often the only ones willing to go into areas too dangerous for anyone from the international community.

Finally, what else do you see in those negotiations that include women? You see a smoother process. The dynamics change in the room when you have men and women working together to move negotiations forward. When I spoke to one of the mediators involved in the Ugandan talks, he said: "Oh, absolutely, it shifted. When we got women in the room, the balance changed." Now there was accountability, and there were people from the communities who had not been there before. Previously you had only the warring parties negotiating with one another as opposed to people who were going to return to their war-torn communities. These women were going to make the negotiators accountable to the people back home. It changed the dynamics and it greased the wheels of the negotiation process.

The evidence is there and, in fact, a recent study was published, actually the first quantitative study addressing the role of women and civil society, and it said peace agreements are more durable when there is a greater degree of openness and a broader extent of participation.

If it's so clear, why it is so hard to make a change? As we can see from the evidence, what is pushing against the seeds of change, against planting them and helping them grow around the world? I think there are three main challenges.

The first is inertia. The vast majority of peace processes today are conducted in a closed room by a male mediator who has been either a political figure somewhere or a mediator previously involved with conflict combatants, with a very limited number of observers, most from third world countries — observer countries. Inertia is a resistance to change, an unwillingness to start seeing things differently and then move in that direction.

The willingness for continuing to do the same thing is backed by an enormous fear of trying to do things differently and failing. It's easier to do the same thing everyone has done before, which has succeeded some percentage of the time than it is to try something completely different. You risk failing and standing out because you didn't do it the way everyone did before that generally worked. It becomes difficult to move institutions, and particularly big bureaucracies, to do things differently when there is no incentive to change the way things have been done in the past.

The second is the fear of the unknown. While there is a potentially greater upside to doing things better, there's a significant downside if it doesn't work. If you don't know what the impact will be of the changes you want to impose, then you worry about unintended consequences. There is a great deal of dialogue when you talk about peace processes and about the risks of bringing other actors into the room. What do I risk by having other people see what I'm doing, how I negotiate, and figure out the shortcomings of the process? Not knowing there is going to be something on the other end that improves what I'm doing creates a lot of fear.

The third challenge is that knowledge is power. The people in those rooms possess all the knowledge and all the power. There is not a single individual in that room who benefits directly from letting others participate. Now, there is a benefit in the long term and a mediator who certainly wants to achieve peace. These folks are there, that's their job, that's what determines whether or not people feel they are worth their paycheck. But until you know it's going to make a difference, it's not enough to give up the information you possess, to give away power for that peace dividend. That's an incredibly strong disincentive to changing the way you build peace today.

So what can we all do? My organization advocates changing the way peace is built, and our advocacy takes several forms. We do tons of research to look at whether it makes a difference, and how it makes a difference. We hold lots of meetings, we bring lots of people to the policymakers who we believe are authentic leaders to have those conversations. But that's fairly technical.

I think there are four things you can do to help us in driving this process forward. The first is to question the status quo. Question the way things are done, question whether or not it could be different and if it could be better, and provide ideas to improve those solutions and continue to ask those questions until it becomes more difficult to keep them the same than it does to change them.

The second is to call for a change in the process. Ask people to do things differently and make it less difficult; make people feel as though they do not have to fight an uphill battle in order to do things another way. Because once people feel there's an opportunity and that people will embrace change, it changes the willingness of those folks to do things differently, to be creative and try different solutions.

The third is to raise the attention and awareness of other participants: women, civil society professionals, academics, service providers, all who are there and are the true constituencies for peace in conflict-ridden societies. Raise this question: Who do you want to build your peace in your society and who do you want to restore that culture of peace? Then force policy makers to think long term about planting those seeds and nurturing them.

Lastly, promulgate and push for the creation of a culture of peace not only in your daily lives and in your jobs, but even in the conversations you have with neighbors when you're talking about the way peace is built. Because, until there is a general recognition that we all need to be involved in returning peace to societies, we are not going to change the way these peace processes are approached and we're not going to leverage the impact and the influence that people like women can have in helping to return peace and prosperity to these cultures all around the world, cultures who otherwise are not leveraging 50 percent of their population in their efforts to end conflict.

I'm probably in the right group when I encourage all of you to take a long look when you're thinking about peacebuilding. We need to change the way people think about the negotiating table, not just think about stopping the fight but think about how the negotiating table builds peace.

When we arrive to where we have a longer term look at the peace negotiation process, we will begin to open the door to the involvement of women and other stakeholders critical to building a culture of peace.

March 3, 2010
SGI-USA Washington, D.C., Culture of Peace Resource Center

Managing Diversity

An Interview With Fathali Moghaddam

Distinguished Professor
Psychology Department and the Conflict Resolution Program
Department of Government
Georgetown University

Fathali Moghaddam is a distinguished professor in the Psychology Department and Conflict Resolution Program, Department of Government at Georgetown University. He was born in Iran, but educated in England from an early age. In the spring of 1979, Dr. Moghaddam traveled back to Iran to conduct research during the hostage-taking crisis and the beginning of the Iran-Iraq War. He began teaching at Georgetown University in 1990 after he worked for the United Nations and McGill University in Canada.

His experimental research, field experience, and extensive publications focus on radicalization, intergroup conflict, human rights and duties, and the psychology of globalization. Dr. Moghaddam's recent publications cover the psychology of dictatorship; pre-emptive duties and rights; and globalization and a conservative dilemma. He is currently working on a new book called the *Psychology of Democracy* and is the editor of *Peace and Conflict: Journal of Peace Psychology*.

Dr. Fathali Moghaddam sat down for an interview in 2014 to discuss the challenges of globalization, managing diversity, and mass immigration with interviewer Victoria Heckenlaible, who is an MA Candidate in the Georgetown Conflict Resolution Program. The interview touches on themes previously explored by Dr. Moghaddam during a 2009 lecture delivered as part of the SGI-USA Culture of Peace Distinguished Speaker Series.

HECKENLAIBLE: During the past few months, American journalists have been beheaded by ISIS, conflicts have escalated in Syria, and violence has increased in the West Bank and Gaza. What are your thoughts on the world's state? Why have we seen an escalation in crises?

MOGHADDAM: It's useful to look at these events in the context of globalization and to think about how globalization is impacting different parts of the world and different collective movements.

HECKENLAIBLE: And what do you mean by the term *globalization*? How has the concept changed over the years?

MOGHADDAM: Globalization is the increasing integration of different societies around the world in terms of economic and cultural connections as well as in terms of security. Globalization today is very different from even twentieth-century globalization. It is being driven by unpredictable technological advances. For example, even in the year 2000, nobody predicted that Twitter and Facebook would transform the social relationships of the young as they have today. This very fast-paced, unpredictable change is bringing people together in a way that is unexpected.

The other aspect of globalization rapidly impacting the globe is the large-scale movement of populations. Mass migration is happening because communities are either refugees or follow emerging labor demands, moving to take advantage of new labor markets. The population shift is concentrated in a movement from Africa and Asia to Western societies. This is particularly prominent in Western Europe and North America where the indigenous populations are not reproducing fast enough to maintain their population levels. In most of Western Europe, the indigenous population is reproducing below 1.2 percent, which is the rate you need to maintain your population level. Because of low birthrates, the European Union, Japan, and others are having to think about importing labor. The EU is not just thinking about it, but actually doing it.

These large-scale population importations then lead to major challenges in organizing societies. Populations arrive with extremely different religions, cultures, and languages than those of the indigenous populations.

HECKENLAIBLE: Which populations are immigrating? Is there a difference between those migrating to Europe versus North America?

MOGHADDAM: Yes, there is. To answer this question, I've put something forward called the "distance traveled hypothesis." It basically says that the distance an immigrant travels for a new host society depends largely on the immigrant's resources. Let's think about the populations moving to the European Union; many are connected through colonial ties. South Asians are going to England, and North Africans are going to France. These populations are not typically highly skilled or greatly resourced. Since they don't have high levels of resources, they reach a country that is closer. But if you are coming from the Middle East to the United States, you are going to need greater resources. So immigrants going to the United States usually have more resources than those going to Western Europe. When we look at the backgrounds of the immigrants and refugees arriving in Europe, we see lower education levels and less resources economically.

HECKENLAIBLE: Beyond resources, how does this affect cultural differences?

MOGHADDAM: This typically means that the immigrants in Europe are more traditional and are more wedded to their heritage languages, cultures, and religions. Assimilation for populations in Europe is going to take longer, especially since North America, Australia, and New Zealand are typically immigrant countries.

HECKENLAIBLE: Could you explain more what you mean by traditional in the context of European immigrants?

MOGHADDAM: Yes, for example, South Asians in England are more wedded to their traditions than the South Asians in North America. You will find that the mosques, the preaching in the mosques, and the style of religiosity are more traditional. Europe has a different challenge because, not only does Europe not have a history of assimilating immigrants as the United States, Canada, New Zealand, and Australia have, but the immigrants arriving in Europe are more traditional. Estimates reveal that anywhere between twenty and thirty million Muslims live in the European Union; this is an example of how large these movements can become. Mass population migration and their characteristics lead us to the challenge of managing diversity.

HECKENLAIBLE: In previous writings, you've mentioned that a reaction to this diversity is assimilation — populations are becoming more Westernized. How does this observation balance with the traditional immigrant populations in Europe?

MOGHADDAM: Globalization does suggest a strategy leading toward integration and homogenization. An example is English. The language has become the language of business and science. Anywhere you go in the business or science community, you use English. At one level, globalization presents a solution to managing diversity, which is to assimilate and to have everyone become the same.

However, it's important to make a distinction between symbolic differences and actual differences. I would argue that in practice homogenization is happening around the world. People's lifestyles are becoming increasingly similar through the spread of consumer products and food styles such as McDonald's and Pizza Hut. People are using the same products and having similar aspirations like wanting a car, a TV, and a washing machine. These are actual similarities. There is also the spreading of values. We know from research that romantic love is spreading around the world as a value. Globally, more people are saying, "I need to fall in love before I get married." This wasn't the case twenty years ago. We also know from research that human rights are spreading even in dictatorships. Values such as elections and voting are spreading to the point that even dictators are forced to hold elections of some kind. Of course, they aren't real elections, but dictators feel like they have to hold elections anyway. While actual differences are decreasing, groups are manufacturing symbolic differences to create a distinct identity for themselves.

HECKENLAIBLE: Why do groups feel the need to manufacture symbolic differences when lifestyles are homogenizing?

MOGHADDAM: Symbolic differences fulfill a psychological need that groups have for a distinct identity. In many cases, groups are reviving old traditions or manufacturing new ones to differentiate themselves. We see movements of separatism, segregation, differentiation, fragmentation. For example, recently a vote was held on Scottish separatism and nationalism. This contrasts with the movement toward assimilation through the European Union. Why would Scotland want to separate? Scottish nationalists would argue that they need to establish their distinct identity and become independent. Today there are many separatist movements reviving their ancient ways, at least symbolically, to establish distinctiveness.

HECKENLAIBLE: But there seems to be a big gap between manufacturing symbolic differences for a distinct identity and fighting over them. What are these potentially conflict-causing differences?

MOGHADDAM: Symbolic differences themselves can serve as a basis for group differentiations in conflict. We know this from historic examples such as Rwanda. The objective differences between a Hutu and Tutsi are very minimal. If you measure the height, there is little difference. One group is supposed to be superior and much taller. These differences are exaggerated by groups to make themselves distinct. During apartheid in South Africa, racial barriers were manufactured. For example, you couldn't tell what racial category some individuals belonged to. Yet they were categorized. People went before official boards to be categorized.

Apart from these historical examples, we also have experimental evidence. The minimal group paradigm is an experiment designed by Henri Tajfel, who placed people in a group on a trivial basis. Within these groups, the members did not know the identity of the others within their group or those in the out-group. They didn't know why they were allocated rewards, and they knew that none of the awards they allocated would come back to them. All the participants knew is that they were in Group X and that somebody else was

in Group Y. Yet typically they showed bias in favor of their group. So
we know that symbolic differences matter.

HECKENLAIBLE: I'm still trying to wrap my mind around how the escalation from identity creation to conflict happens. Could you clarify
the process?

MOGHADDAM: Categorizing the world into "us" and "them" is a basic
step toward conflict. The categorization creates a situation where you
say: "We are the good people, and they are the evil ones. We as the
good people have to exterminate the evil ones." Unfortunately, history provides us with many examples of these attempts to annihilate
the "other." Many groups who used to exist don't anymore. Thousands of languages have been wiped out.

But now to your question, what transitions us into fighting?
There are several potential explanations. Social biology argues that
we are genetically programmed to perpetuate our genes and to wipe
out other competing gene pools. While the explanation has some
merit, I don't believe it explains the current situation in the world.

The materialist approach states that we are actually fighting over
resources as selfish and egocentric creatures. Our fighting is really
about land, oil, minerals, and resources. Again, I think this explanation is too simplistic, because if we were really trying to maximize our profits, we could do so often without fighting. Think about
the Iraq Invasion in 2003. The United States led that invasion. Since
then, estimates are that the United States has spent three to four trillion dollars on the invasion. If the United States was really after oil,
it could have bought a lot of oil on the open market for three or four
trillion dollars. The United States has not gotten out of that situation
what it has spent.

A third explanation comes from the school of thought that says
humans are irrational and aggressive. We don't know what drives
our own behavior. We get into wars for irrational reasons and then
rationalize our aggression. We claim that we've been fighting for
peace, for democracy, or for land. But we are driven to fight by factors beyond our own consciousness.

Other theories about why we fight focus on justice and relative
deprivation, that is, the idea that we fight because we feel deprived

relative to others. In reality, the reason we fight is probably a combination of these explanations. Human history demonstrates that we fall into this violent trap again and again. We continue to inflict pain, suffering, and death on other people. And this is a cycle we are having a tough time getting out of.

HECKENLAIBLE: How has globalization impacted this process? Has it expedited the violence?

MOGHADDAM: Yes, I have argued that globalization is a major factor that has led to radicalization and terrorism. This process is spurred on by Sudden Contact Theory, which I borrowed from biologists such as Paul Ehrlich. Catastrophic evolution, which involves Sudden Contact Theory, is the idea that, when different plants and animals come together without preadaptation, the local species is often wiped out. Sometimes this takes place rapidly.

I have argued that the same thing happens in the human world. A human group moves in large numbers and comes into contact with another human group without preadaptation. The result is that the local populations are wiped out. You may ask, "Has this ever happened in human history?" Well, just look at North and South America. The estimates state that up to one hundred million people lived in North and South America until the local populations were wiped out by Western colonizers. How did this happen? Mostly through disease rather than direct violence. But it was violence of one kind or another.

HECKENLAIBLE: Is Sudden Contact Theory mostly linked with disease? Or can it be applied more broadly?

MOGHADDAM: It is not limited to disease. Social Contact Theory involves the wiping out of lifestyles, languages, and cultures, so that you gradually get homogenization around the world.

HECKENLAIBLE: So in reaction to Social Contact Theory and globalization, how have countries and governments responded?

MOGHADDAM: Countries and regions have reacted very differently to this problem. Traditional immigrant receiving countries like America, Canada, Australia, and New Zealand have always had the challenge of managing diversity at the forefront. However, Western European countries as well as Japan must now grapple with the challenge because they need a larger labor force. Countries have responded through different diversity management approaches. The question is, how do you manage diversity when the immigrant population is not from traditional European sources?

HECKENLAIBLE: And, to clarify, how exactly do you define managing diversity?

MOGHADDAM: It means, how do we treat cultural and linguistic differences. Do we assume that societies should assimilate and become more similar? Will the minority culture merge into the majority? Or do we assume that it is a better policy if minorities maintain their heritage cultures and languages? Should the government support this diversity and differences in language and culture? How do these policies lead us toward celebrating diversity or toward greater unification?

North America has typically been an immigrant receiving country. Everyone has immigrant roots minus the native peoples, who were unfortunately wiped out. We can think of the United States and Canada as lands of immigrants. Prior to World War II, most of the immigrants that came to Canada and the United States were from Western European countries like Ireland, Italy, Spain, and Germany. But, after World War II, there was a shift. Birth rates dropped in Western Europe, while birth rates increased in Asia and Africa due to improved healthcare and nutrition. This caused a shift in the sources of immigrants going to North America. The new immigrants from Asia and Africa were often not from the same Christian, European, white background as mainstream America. They were often phenotypically different from white Americans. The immigrants had different food habits and spoke different languages. The challenge has been to integrate these new, very different immigrants.

Starting in the 1970s, Canada adopted a multicultural policy. Prime Minister Pierre Elliot Trudeau introduced it in the early 1970s. By the late 1970s, Canadian multiculturalism became official government policy that provided state support for minority groups, languages, and cultures. At its heart is the multiculturalism hypothesis. This assumes that, if we help people feel confident and take pride in their heritage cultures, they will be accepting toward others. Minorities will share their cultures with others, and be willing to understand other cultures. This seems like a benevolent constructive approach.

However, my colleagues and I found that the relationship between pride in a heritage culture and being accepting is incredibly complicated. We actually presented our research to Trudeau, and the research wasn't as he expected. Historically, there have been many groups like the Nazis who took pride in their heritage, but were not open to others. Trudeau was very interested in this point and the research, but as a politician, he was using multiculturalism to deal with a political problem. His policies focused on bilingualism between French and English. But he was stuck with other cultures saying, "What about our languages?" To appease them, he offered multiculturalism, though many researchers have found that multiculturalism has challenges. In fact, within the past few years, the heads of state in Germany, England, and France all declared that multiculturalism failed in their countries. And I believe it failed in North America as well.

HECKENLAIBLE: What evidence do you have outside of your initial research that it has failed?

MOGHADDAM: When we look at the performance of minorities in the education system, it has not improved despite multiculturalist policies. Instead, the policies have actually hindered minorities by encouraging them to compete outside the mainstream. The Canadian multiculturalism policies are what I call "folk dance multiculturalism." The government supports the celebrations of local traditions, but again, does not help minorities compete. Minorities still retain heritage languages, but the performance of minorities in the Canada system and social mobility hasn't changed. Canadian society is still very hierarchical with the white majority in the lead.

Multiculturalism is very good rhetoric, and it makes for a good story. But actual facts question it. The question is, how do you get people and politicians to rethink multiculturalism in a time when it is politically correct?

HECKENLAIBLE: Then, how do we encourage the debate? What are the barriers to discussion?

MOGHADDAM: One of the challenges in encouraging more debate is that multiculturalism is strongly supported by the elites within minority groups. They benefit from this policy. If you happen to be a politician with a base consisting of mostly Group X, you certainly don't want Group X weakened. You want Group X to think of themselves as different. You want them to think of you as their representative and to vote according to the block that serves your purpose. As it exists today, multiculturalism is self-serving for the elites within minorities. This creates a big political challenge to questioning the polities.

Challenging the policy is also tricky for politicians. No one dares question it, even in an education system where critical thinking is espoused. It has become the politically correct theory because minorities have bought into the story that multiculturalism works in their favor. Therefore, the rethinking of diversity management policies must come from the minorities themselves. They have yet to realize that the present system does not serve their purposes.

We must encourage discussion through asking questions similar to these, publicizing opinions, and waiting for minorities to ask: "Why are our children failing? What is underlying this?" I think once people seriously ask these questions, policies will change.

HECKENLAIBLE: After people start questioning multiculturalism, where do you propose future diversity management policies should go?

MOGHADDAM: The traditional solution has been assimilation. That has been tried and has major flaws. Minorities do not want to wholeheartedly take up the model of the mainstream. They want something separate. Other policies like polyculturalism have been proposed. Historians that argue this approach say that all cultures have the same root.

I have put forward the idea of omniculturalism, which covers two stages. During stage one, which lasts until the early teens, children are taught human commonalities. This is in response to the question, "What is a human being?" Their first task is to answer that question. Once that is achieved, students go to the second phase, which recognizes the differences. The celebration of differences comes after people have learned humans have fundamental similarities. This results in the omnicultural imperative. When you are interacting with anyone, your first socialized impulse should be, "What are the commonalities between us?" It should not be the impulse that first asks, "What are the differences between us?"

We should socialize human beings to think commonalities first and then understand the differences.

While I do think we should consider omniculturalism as a policy, it's just one of the many possibilities. My main goal is to encourage people to rethink current practices.

HECKENLAIBLE: Interesting. Thank you very much, Dr. Moghaddam, for this conversation and raising these important questions.

MOGHADDAM: Of course, managing diversity and conflict is a crucial subject.

October/November 2014
Georgetown University

APPENDIX A

DECLARATION ON A CULTURE OF PEACE

United Nations Fifty-third Session Agenda Item 31: Resolutions Adopted by the General Assembly

The General Assembly,

Recalling the *Charter of the United Nations,* including the purposes and principles embodied therein,

Recalling also the *Constitution of the United Nations Educational, Scientific and Cultural Organization,* which states that "since wars begin in the minds of men, it is in the minds of men that the defences of peace must be constructed,"

Recalling further the *Universal Declaration of Human Rights*[1] and other relevant international instruments of the United Nations system,

Recognizing that peace not only is the absence of conflict, but also requires a positive, dynamic participatory process where dialogue is encouraged and conflicts are solved in a spirit of mutual understanding and cooperation,

Recognizing also that the end of the cold war has widened possibilities for strengthening a culture of peace,

Expressing deep concern about the persistence and proliferation of violence and conflict in various parts of the world,

Recognizing the need to eliminate all forms of discrimination and intolerance, including those based on race, colour, sex, language, religion, political or other opinion, national, ethnic or social origin, property, disability, birth or other status,

Recalling its *resolution 52/15* of 20 November 1997, by which it proclaimed the year 2000 as the "International Year for the Culture of Peace," and its *resolution 53/25* of 10 November 1998, by which it proclaimed the period

2001–2010 as the "International Decade for a Culture of Peace and Non-Violence for the Children of the World,"

Recognizing the important role that the United Nations Educational, Scientific and Cultural Organization continues to play in the promotion of a culture of peace,

Solemnly proclaims the present Declaration on a Culture of Peace to the end that Governments, international organizations and civil society may be guided in their activity by its provisions to promote and strengthen a culture of peace in the new millennium:

ARTICLE 1

A culture of peace is a set of values, attitudes, traditions and modes of behaviour and ways of life based on:

(*a*) Respect for life, ending of violence and promotion and practice of non-violence through education, dialogue and cooperation;

(*b*) Full respect for the principles of sovereignty, territorial integrity and political independence of States and non-intervention in matters which are essentially within the domestic jurisdiction of any State, in accordance with the Charter of the United Nations and international law;

(*c*) Full respect for and promotion of all human rights and fundamental freedoms;

(*d*) Commitment to peaceful settlement of conflicts;

(*e*) Efforts to meet the developmental and environmental needs of present and future generations;

(*f*) Respect for and promotion of the right to development;

(*g*) Respect for and promotion of equal rights and opportunities for women and men;

(*h*) Respect for and promotion of the right of everyone to freedom of expression, opinion and information;

(*i*) Adherence to the principles of freedom, justice, democracy, tolerance, solidarity, cooperation, pluralism, cultural diversity, dialogue and understanding at all levels of society and among nations; and fostered by an enabling national and international environment conducive to peace.

ARTICLE 2

Progress in the fuller development of a culture of peace comes about through values, attitudes, modes of behaviour and ways of life conducive to the promotion of peace among individuals, groups and nations.

ARTICLE 3

The fuller development of a culture of peace is integrally linked to:

(*a*) Promoting peaceful settlement of conflicts, mutual respect and understanding and international cooperation;

(*b*) Complying with international obligations under the Charter of the United Nations and international law;

(*c*) Promoting democracy, development and universal respect for and observance of all human rights and fundamental freedoms;

(*d*) Enabling people at all levels to develop skills of dialogue, negotiation, consensus-building and peaceful resolution of differences;

(*e*) Strengthening democratic institutions and ensuring full participation in the development process;

(*f*) Eradicating poverty and illiteracy and reducing inequalities within and among nations;

(*g*) Promoting sustainable economic and social development;

(*h*) Eliminating all forms of discrimination against women through their empowerment and equal representation at all levels of decision-making;

(*i*) Ensuring respect for and promotion and protection of the rights of children;

(*j*) Ensuring free flow of information at all levels and enhancing access thereto;

(*k*) Increasing transparency and accountability in governance;

(*l*) Eliminating all forms of racism, racial discrimination, xenophobia and related intolerance;

(*m*) Advancing understanding, tolerance and solidarity among all civilizations, peoples and cultures, including towards ethnic, religious and linguistic minorities;

(*n*) Realizing fully the right of all peoples, including those living under colonial or other forms of alien domination or foreign occupation, to self-determination enshrined in the Charter of the United Nations and embodied in the International Covenants on Human Rights,[2] as well as in the Declaration on the Granting of Independence to Colonial Countries and Peoples contained in General Assembly resolution 1514 (XV) of 14 December 1960.

ARTICLE 4

Education at all levels is one of the principal means to build a culture of peace. In this context, human rights education is of particular importance.

ARTICLE 5

Governments have an essential role in promoting and strengthening a culture of peace.

ARTICLE 6

Civil society needs to be fully engaged in fuller development of a culture of peace.

ARTICLE 7

The educative and informative role of the media contributes to the promotion of a culture of peace.

ARTICLE 8

A key role in the promotion of a culture of peace belongs to parents, teachers, politicians, journalists, religious bodies and groups, intellectuals, those engaged in scientific, philosophical and creative and artistic activities, health and humanitarian workers, social workers, managers at various levels as well as to non-governmental organizations.

ARTICLE 9

The United Nations should continue to play a critical role in the promotion and strengthening of a culture of peace worldwide.

107th plenary meeting
13 September 1999

1. Resolution 217A (III)
2. Resolution 2200A (XXI), annex.

APPENDIX B

PROGRAMME OF ACTION ON A CULTURE OF PEACE

United Nations Fifty-third Session Agenda Item 31

The General Assembly,

Bearing in mind the Declaration on a Culture of Peace adopted on 13 September 1999,

Recalling its *resolution 52/15* of 20 November 1997, by which it proclaimed the year 2000 as the "International Year for the Culture of Peace," and its *resolution 53/25* of 10 November 1998, by which it proclaimed the period 2001–2010 as the "International Decade for a Culture of Peace and Non-violence for the Children of the World";

Adopts the following Programme of Action on a Culture of Peace:

A. AIMS, STRATEGIES AND MAIN ACTORS

1. The Programme of Action should serve as the basis for the International Year for the Culture of Peace and the International Decade for a Culture of Peace and Non-violence for the Children of the World.

2. Member States are encouraged to take actions for promoting a culture of peace at the national level as well as at the regional and international levels.

3. Civil society should be involved at the local, regional and national levels to widen the scope of activities on a culture of peace.

4. The United Nations system should strengthen its ongoing efforts to promote a culture of peace.

5. The United Nations Educational, Scientific and Cultural Organization should continue to play its important role in and make major contributions to the promotion of a culture of peace.

6. Partnerships between and among the various actors as set out in the Declaration should be encouraged and strengthened for a global movement for a culture of peace.

7. A culture of peace could be promoted through sharing of information among actors on their initiatives in this regard.

8. Effective implementation of the Programme of Action requires mobilization of resources, including financial resources, by interested Governments, organizations and individuals.

B. STRENGTHENING ACTIONS AT THE NATIONAL, REGIONAL AND INTERNATIONAL LEVELS BY ALL RELEVANT ACTORS

9. Actions to foster a culture of peace through education:

   (*a*) Reinvigorate national efforts and international cooperation to promote the goals of education for all with a view to achieving human, social and economic development and for promoting a culture of peace;

   (*b*) Ensure that children, from an early age, benefit from education on the values, attitudes, modes of behaviour and ways of life to enable them to resolve any dispute peacefully and in a spirit of respect for human dignity and of tolerance and non-discrimination;

   (*c*) Involve children in activities designed to instill in them the values and goals of a culture of peace;

   (*d*) Ensure equality of access to education for women, especially girls;

   (*e*) Encourage revision of educational curricula, including textbooks, bearing in mind the 1995 Declaration and Integrated Framework of Action on Education for Peace, Human Rights and Democracy[1] for which technical cooperation should be provided by the United Nations Educational, Scientific and Cultural Organization upon request;

   (*f*) Encourage and strengthen efforts by actors as identified in the

Declaration, in particular the United Nations Educational, Scientific and Cultural Organization, aimed at developing values and skills conducive to a culture of peace, including education and training in promoting dialogue and consensus-building;

(*g*) Strengthen the ongoing efforts of the relevant entities of the United Nations system aimed at training and education, where appropriate, in the areas of conflict prevention and crisis management, peaceful settlement of disputes, as well as in post-conflict peace-building;

(*h*) Expand initiatives to promote a culture of peace undertaken by institutions of higher education in various parts of the world, including the United Nations University, the University for Peace and the project for twinning universities and the United Nations Educational, Scientific and Cultural Organization Chairs Programme.

10. Actions to promote sustainable economic and social development:

(*a*) Undertake comprehensive actions on the basis of appropriate strategies and agreed targets to eradicate poverty through national and international efforts, including through international cooperation;

(*b*) Strengthen the national capacity for implementation of policies and programmes designed to reduce economic and social inequalities within nations through, *inter alia*, international cooperation;

(*c*) Promote effective and equitable development-oriented and durable solutions to the external debt and debt-servicing problems of developing countries through, *inter alia*, debt relief;

(*d*) Reinforce actions at all levels to implement national strategies for sustainable food security, including the development of actions to mobilize and optimize the allocation and utilization of resources from all sources, including through international cooperation, such as resources coming from debt relief;

(*e*) Undertake further efforts to ensure that the development process is participatory and that development projects involve the full participation of all;

(*f*) Include a gender perspective and empowerment of women and girls as an integral part of the development process;

(*g*) Include in development strategies special measures focusing on needs of women and children as well as groups with special needs;

(*h*) Strengthen, through development assistance in post-conflict situations, rehabilitation, reintegration and reconciliation processes involving all engaged in conflicts;

(*i*) Incorporate capacity-building in development strategies and projects to ensure environmental sustainability, including preservation and regeneration of the natural resource base;

(*j*) Remove obstacles to the realization of the right of peoples to self-determination, in particular of peoples living under colonial or other forms of alien domination or foreign occupation, which adversely affect their social and economic development.

11. Actions to promote respect for all human rights:

(*a*) Full implementation of the Vienna Declaration and Programme of Action;[2]

(*b*) Encouragement of development of national plans of action for the promotion and protection of all human rights;

(*c*) Strengthening of national institutions and capacities in the field of human rights, including through national human rights institutions;

(*d*) Realization and implementation of the right to development, as established in the Declaration on the Right to Development[3] and the Vienna Declaration and Programme of Action;

(*e*) Achievement of the goals of the United Nations Decade for Human Rights Education (1995–2004);[4]

(*f*) Dissemination and promotion of the Universal Declaration of Human Rights at all levels;

(*g*) Further support to the activities of the United Nations High Commissioner for Human Rights in the fulfilment of her or his mandate as established in General Assembly resolution 48/141 of 20 December 1993, as well as the responsibilities set by subsequent resolutions and decisions.

12. Actions to ensure equality between women and men:

(*a*) Integration of a gender perspective into the implementation of all relevant international instruments;

(*b*) Further implementation of international instruments that promote equality between women and men;

(*c*) Implementation of the Beijing Platform for Action adopted at the Fourth World Conference on Women,[5] with adequate resources and political will, and through, *inter alia*, the elaboration, implementation and follow-up of the national plans of action;

(*d*) Promotion of equality between women and men in economic, social and political decision-making;

(*e*) Further strengthening of efforts by the relevant entities of the United Nations system for the elimination of all forms of discrimination and violence against women;

(*f*) Provision of support and assistance to women who have become victims of any forms of violence, including in the home, workplace and during armed conflicts.

13. Actions to foster democratic participation:

(*a*) Reinforcement of the full range of actions to promote democratic principles and practices;

(*b*) Special emphasis on democratic principles and practices at all levels of formal, informal and non-formal education;

(*c*) Establishment and strengthening of national institutions and processes that promote and sustain democracy through, *inter alia*, training and capacity-building of public officials;

(*d*) Strengthening of democratic participation through, *inter alia*, the provision of electoral assistance upon the request of States concerned and based on relevant United Nations guidelines;

(*e*) Combating of terrorism, organized crime, corruption as well as production, trafficking and consumption of illicit drugs and money laundering, as they undermine democracies and impede the fuller development of a culture of peace.

14. Actions to advance understanding, tolerance and solidarity:

(*a*) Implement the Declaration of Principles on Tolerance and the Follow-up Plan of Action for the United Nations Year for Tolerance[6] (1995);

(*b*) Support activities in the context of the United Nations Year of Dialogue among Civilizations in the year 2001;

(*c*) Study further the local or indigenous practices and traditions of dispute settlement and promotion of tolerance with the objective of learning from them;

(*d*) Support actions that foster understanding, tolerance and solidarity throughout society, in particular with vulnerable groups;

(*e*) Further support the attainment of the goals of the International Decade of the World's Indigenous People;

(*f*) Support actions that foster tolerance and solidarity with refugees and displaced persons, bearing in mind the objective of facilitating their voluntary return and social integration;

(*g*) Support actions that foster tolerance and solidarity with migrants;

(*h*) Promote increased understanding, tolerance and cooperation among all peoples through, *inter alia*, appropriate use of new technologies and dissemination of information;

(*i*) Support actions that foster understanding, tolerance, solidarity and cooperation among peoples and within and among nations.

15. Actions to support participatory communication and the free flow of information and knowledge:

    (*a*) Support the important role of the media in the promotion of a culture of peace;

    (*b*) Ensure freedom of the press and freedom of information and communication;

    (*c*) Make effective use of the media for advocacy and dissemination of information on a culture of peace involving, as appropriate, the United Nations and relevant regional, national and local mechanisms;

    (*d*) Promote mass communication that enables communities to express their needs and participate in decision-making;

    (*e*) Take measures to address the issue of violence in the media, including new communication technologies, *inter alia*, the Internet;

    (*f*) Increase efforts to promote the sharing of information on new information technologies, including the Internet.

16. Actions to promote international peace and security:

    (*a*) Promote general and complete disarmament under strict and effective international control, taking into account the priorities established by the United Nations in the field of disarmament;

    (*b*) Draw, where appropriate, on lessons conducive to a culture of peace learned from "military conversion" efforts as evidenced in some countries of the world;

    (*c*) Emphasize the inadmissibility of acquisition of territory by war and the need to work for a just and lasting peace in all parts of the world;

    (*d*) Encourage confidence-building measures and efforts for negotiating peaceful settlements;

    (*e*) Take measures to eliminate illicit production and traffic of small arms and light weapons;

(*f*) Support initiatives, at the national, regional and international levels, to address concrete problems arising from post-conflict situations, such as demobilization, reintegration of former combatants into society, as well as refugees and displaced persons, weapon collection programmes, exchange of information and confidence-building;

(*g*) Discourage the adoption of and refrain from any unilateral measure, not in accordance with international law and the Charter of the United Nations, that impedes the full achievement of economic and social development by the population of the affected countries, in particular women and children, that hinders their well-being, that creates obstacles to the full enjoyment of their human rights, including the right of everyone to a standard of living adequate for their health and well-being and their right to food, medical care and the necessary social services, while reaffirming that food and medicine must not be used as a tool for political pressure;

(*h*) Refrain from military, political, economic or any other form of coercion, not in accordance with international law and the Charter, aimed against the political independence or territorial integrity of any State;

(*i*) Recommend proper consideration for the issue of the humanitarian impact of sanctions, in particular on women and children, with a view to minimizing the humanitarian effects of sanctions;

(*j*) Promote greater involvement of women in prevention and resolution of conflicts and, in particular, in activities promoting a culture of peace in post-conflict situations;

(*k*) Promote initiatives in conflict situations such as days of tranquillity to carry out immunization and medicine distribution campaigns, corridors of peace to ensure delivery of humanitarian supplies and sanctuaries of peace to respect the central role of health and medical institutions such as hospitals and clinics;

(*l*) Encourage training in techniques for the understanding, prevention and resolution of conflict for the concerned staff of the United Nations, relevant regional organizations and Member States, upon request, where appropriate.

107th plenary meeting
13 September 1999

1. United Nations Educational, Scientific and Cultural Organization, *Records of the General Conference, Twenty-eighth Session, Paris, 25 October–16 November 1995*, vol. 1: Resolutions, resolution 5.4, annexes.

2. A/CONF.157/24 (Part I), chap. III.

3. Resolution 41/128, annex.

4. See A/49/261-E/1994/110/Add.1, annex.

5. *Report of the Fourth World Conference on Women, Beijing, 4–15 September 1995* (United Nations publication, Sales No. E.96.IV.13), chap. I, resolution 1, annex II.

6. A/51/201, appendix I.

APPENDIX C

UNITED NATIONS RESOLUTIONS AND OTHER REFERENCE DOCUMENTS ON A CULTURE OF PEACE

A/RES/62/39   International Decade for a Culture of Peace and Non-Violence for the Children of the World, 2001–2010, Adopted 17 December 2007
www.un.org/Docs/journal/asp/ws.asp?m=A/RES/62/89

A/RES/61/45   same as above, Adopted 4 December 2006
www.un.org/Docs/journal/asp/ws.asp?m=A/RES/61/45

A/RES/59/143 same as above, Adopted 15 December 2004
www.un.org/Docs/journal/asp/ws.asp?m=A/RES/59/143

A/RES/58/11   same as above, Adopted 10 November 2003
www.un.org/Docs/journal/asp/ws.asp?m=A/RES/58/11

A/RES/57/6   same as above, Adopted 4 November 2002
www.un.org/Docs/journal/asp/ws.asp?m=A/RES/57/6

A/RES/56/5   same as above, Adopted 5 November 2001
www.un.org/Docs/journal/asp/ws.asp?m=A/RES/56/5

A/RES/55/47   same as above, Adopted 29 November 2000
www.un.org/Docs/journal/asp/ws.asp?m=A/RES/55/47

A/RES/53/25   same as above, Adopted 10 November 1998
www.un.org/Docs/journal/asp/ws.asp?m=A/RES/53/25

A/RES/52/13   Culture of Peace, Adopted 20 November 1997
www.un.org/Docs/journal/asp/ws.asp?m=A/RES/52/13

E/1997/47   International Year for the Culture of Peace, 2000, Adopted 22 July 1997

ap.ohchr.org/documents/E/ECOSOC/resolutions/
E-RES-1997-47.doc

OTHER REPORTS

A/62/97   International Decade for a Culture of Peace and Non-Violence for the Children of the World (2001–2010), Note by the Secretary-General, Issued 28 June 2007
www.un.org/Docs/journal/asp/ws.asp?m=A/62/97

A/61/175   Culture of Peace, Notes by the Secretary-General, Issued 24 July 2006
www.un.org/Docs/journal/asp/ws.asp?m=A/61/175

A/60/279   Midterm global review of the International Decade for a Culture of Peace and Non-Violence for the Children of the World, 2001-2010, Issued 19 August 2005
www.un.org/Docs/journal/asp/ws.asp?m=A/60/279

A/59/223   International Decade for a Culture of Peace and Non-Violence for the Children of the World (2001–2010), Note by the Secretary-General, Issued 10 August 2004
www.un.org/Docs/journal/asp/ws.asp?m=A/59/223

A/58/182   International Decade for a Culture of Peace and Non-Violence for the Children of the World (2001–2010), Note by the Secretary-General, Issued 24 July 2003
www.un.org/Docs/journal/asp/ws.asp?m=A/58/182

A/57/186   International Decade for a Culture of Peace and Non-Violence for the Children of the World, Implementation of General Assembly resolution 56/5, Note by the Secretary-General, Issued 2 July 2002
www.un.org/Docs/journal/asp/ws.asp?m=A/57/186

A/56/349   International Decade for a Culture of Peace and Non-Violence for the Children of the World, 2001–2010, Report of the Secretary-General, Issued 13 September 2001
www.un.org/Docs/journal/asp/ws.asp?m=A/56/349

A/55/377   International Decade for a Culture of Peace and Non-Violence for the Children of the World, 2001–2010,

Report of the Secretary-General, Issued 12 September
2000
www.un.org/Docs/journal/asp/ws.asp?m=A/55/377

OTHER REFERENCE DOCUMENTS

World Report on the Culture of Peace

Civil Society report at midpoint of the Culture of Peace Decade,
Issued 2005
decade-culture-of-peace.org/report/wrcpx.pdf

APPENDIX D

ABOUT THE SGI-USA CULTURE OF PEACE RESOURCE CENTERS

The SGI-USA is involved in non-sectarian, public awareness activities to promote the values of peace, culture, and education and works with other civil-society and nongovernmental groups to develop youth programs, traveling exhibits, cultural events, and symposia.

For more information, go to www.sgi-usa.org.

Santa Monica Culture of Peace Resource Center
SGI Plaza
606 Wilshire Boulevard, Santa Monica, CA 90401

Chicago Culture of Peace Resource Center
SGI-USA Chicago Culture Center
1455 South Wabash Avenue, Chicago, IL 60605

New York Culture of Peace Resource Center
SGI-USA New York Culture Center
7 East 15th Street, New York, NY 10003

Honolulu Culture of Peace Resource Center
SGI-USA Hawaii Culture Center
2729 Pali Highway, Honolulu, HI 96817

Washington, D.C., Culture of Peace Resource Center
SGI-USA Washington, D.C., Buddhist Center
3417 Massachusetts Avenue, Washington, D.C. 20007

San Francisco Culture of Peace Resource Center
SGI-USA San Francisco Culture Center
2450 17th Street, San Francisco, CA 94110

INDEX

ability, increased by effort, 78, 80, 98
accountability, 62, 157
Achebe, Chinua, 10
action, xvi, 26, 31-32, 43, 78, 81, 85, 91-92, 96, 98
activism, 94, 96-97
Aegean Sea, 142
Afghanistan, 8, 50, 69, 73-74; women in, 156
Affirmative Action, 77
Africa, 10, 15, 21, 26, 69, 73, 106, 115, 162, 168; freedom of press in, 104; partnership with, 28-31
African American, 88
Agriculture Labor Relations Act, 91
Ahmadinejad, 134
al-Bashir, Omar, 51-52, 64-65
Alinsky, Saul, 84
American Psychiatric Association, 18
appreciation, 11
Arbour, Louise, 59
Arendt, Hannah, 60, 64-65
Aristotle, 122
Arizona, 91
Armistice Day, 129-30
Asia, 73, 115, 162, 168
Australia, 163-64
awareness, 158

Bahamas, xiv
Bailey, Bobby, 43
Baldwin, James, 72
Ban Ki-moon, ix, xvi, 39
Beah, Ishmael, 1; as a member of the Human Rights Watch Children's Rights Division Committee, 2

Begin, Menachem, 132
Bhutan, xiv
Bling the Planet Rock (film), 16
Blood Diamond (film), 14, 30
Bohm, David, 120
Bosnia, 65; peace process in, 154; war in, 52-53, 55-56
Boutwell, Jeffrey, as executive director of the Pugwash Conferences on Science and World Affairs, 129-30
Bowling Alone (Putnam), 140
Brazil, 8, 135
Britain, 130, 135
Bruno, Giordiano, 122
Burma (Myanmar), 50
Butler, Sean, 57

California, 91
Cambodia, 56-57, 59, 65
Cameroon, 19
Camp David Accord, 132
Canada, 138, 164, 167-68
Capitol Hill [Washington, D.C.], 42
Carter, Jimmy, 129
Cassese, Antonio, 62-63
Centenary Methodist Church (Memphis), 67
Central African Republic, 40, 57
Central Asia, 69
Cepeda, Raquel, 16
challenge, spirit of, xv, 32, 44
change, challenges against, 157-58; potential to, 32, 35-37, 41, 43-45, 78, 80, 82, 85-87, 90-91, 98, 113-14, 117-18, 125

Printed in Great Britain
by Amazon